Managing and Optimizing VMware vSphere® Deployments

D1616730

VMware Press is the official publisher of VMware books and training materials, which provide guidance on the critical topics facing today's technology professionals and students. Enterprises, as well as small- and medium-sized organizations, adopt virtualization as a more agile way of scaling IT to meet business needs. VMware Press provides proven, technically accurate information that will help them meet their goals for customizing, building, and maintaining their virtual environment.

With books, certification and study guides, video training, and learning tools produced by world-class architects and IT experts, VMware Press helps IT professionals master a diverse range of topics on virtualization and cloud computing and is the official source of reference materials for preparing for the VMware Certified Professional Examination.

VMware Press is also pleased to have localization partners that can publish its products into more than 42 languages, including, but not limited to, Chinese (Simplified), Chinese (Traditional), French, German, Greek, Hindi, Japanese, Korean, Polish, Russian, and Spanish.

For more information about VMware Press, please visit
http://www.vmware.com/go/vmwarepress

Managing and Optimizing VMware vSphere® Deployments

Sean Crookston
Harley Stagner

vmware® PRESS

Upper Saddle River, NJ • Boston • Indianapolis • San Francisco
New York • Toronto • Montreal • London • Munich • Paris • Madrid
Cape Town • Sydney • Tokyo • Singapore • Mexico City

Managing and Optimizing VMware vSphere Deployments

Published by Pearson Education, Inc.

Publishing as VMware Press

ISBN-10: 0-321-82047-9

ISBN-13: 978-0-321-82047-1

Library of Congress Cataloging-in-Publication data is on file.

Printed in the United States of America

First Printing: July 2012

All terms mentioned in this book that are known to be trademarks or service marks have been appropriately capitalized. The publisher cannot attest to the accuracy of this information. Use of a term in this book should not be regarded as affecting the validity of any trademark or service mark.

VMware terms are trademarks or registered trademarks of VMware in the United States, other countries, or both.

Warning and Disclaimer

Corporate and Government Sales

VMware Press offers excellent discounts on this book when ordered in quantity for bulk purchases or special sales, which may include electronic versions and/or custom covers and content particular to your business, training goals, marketing focus, and branding interests. For more information, please contact:

U.S. Corporate and Government Sales
(800) 382-3419
corpsales@pearsontechgroup.com

For sales outside the United States please contact:

International Sales
international@pearson.com

VMWARE PRESS

PROGRAM MANAGER
Erik Ullanderson

ASSOCIATE PUBLISHER
David Dusthimer

EDITOR
Joan Murray

DEVELOPMENT EDITOR
Ellie Bru

MANAGING EDITOR
Sandra Schroeder

SENIOR PROJECT EDITOR
Tonya Simpson

COPY EDITOR
Karen Annett

PROOFREADER
Debbie Williams

INDEXER
Tim Wright

EDITORIAL ASSISTANT
Vanessa Evans

BOOK DESIGNER
Gary Adair

COMPOSITOR
Bronkella Publishing

Sean Crookston—I would like to dedicate this book to my wife and son. Without their support this book would not have been possible.

Harley Stagner—I would like to dedicate this book to my wife, Kimberly. Her infinite supply of support and patience during this process made this book possible.

Contents

Preface

In our experience as consultants, VMware vSphere is the most robust virtualization solution on the market. The technology is proven and the user base is large.

Although the benefits of virtualization using vSphere are many, proper planning is required to gain these benefits from a vSphere infrastructure. This book is a guide to planning, designing, implementing, operating, and managing a robust vSphere infrastructure. The best practices and advice given in this book come from our own extensive field experience as datacenter architects and implementation engineers.

We wrote this book after noticing a need for the above mentioned areas. Many VMware books tell you how to set up and configure vSphere, but few talk about specific and real use cases. This book provides an in-depth discussion of business drivers and decisions around virtualization, an area that is not often covered.

Authors' Disclaimer

Although we have made every effort possible, we assume no responsibility for errors or omissions. Neither is any liability assumed for damages resulting from the use of information contained in this book.

You the Reader

This book is intended for systems administrators with experience using VMware's vSphere products. The products discussed in this book include vSphere, vCenter Operations, VMware Data Recovery, VMware View, VMware Site Recovery Manager, and other third-party additions, such as the Cisco Nexus 1000v distributed virtual switch. While we do expect this level of experience, we have noted resources for further research and learning in Appendix A where appropriate.

What This Book Covers

Here is a quick rundown of what is covered in *Managing and Optimizing VMware vSphere Deployments*:

Chapter 1, "Laying the Groundwork"

This chapter talks about building a proper foundation for the virtual infrastructure. Many of the design considerations and best practices that show up in later chapters are mentioned here. These decisions will serve as the foundation for a design blueprint.

Chapter 2, "Implementing the Solution"

This chapter talks about the considerations when implementing a vSphere-based solution. You learn the process of taking a design from the blueprint and bringing it to completion through the implementation process.

Chapter 3, "Operating the Environment"

This chapter talks about operating a vSphere-based solution. It discusses many of the day-to-day tasks that are sometimes overlooked and provides some great community resources for aiding in these tasks.

Chapter 4, "Managing the Environment"

This chapter talks about managing a vSphere-based solution after the implementation. It discusses both capacity and performance management. It also looks at how capacity planning and forecasting can be used on an ongoing basis as the infrastructure grows.

Chapter 5, "Roadblocks to 100% Virtualization"

This chapter talks about the journey toward 100% virtualization. You learn the roadblocks that prevent many organizations from continuing virtualization initiatives and what can be done to help facilitate breaking through these stall points.

Chapter 6, "Full Case Study"

This chapter brings what you have learned together in a customer case study. You explore a design from its inception to the implementation. You then explore the reasons for the design decisions along the way.

Appendix A, "Additional Resources"

This appendix includes a list of resources and learning materials mentioned throughout the book to aid the reader in further research.

Hyperlinks

When necessary, we have provided resources in the appendix of this book to Internet resources that aid or speak further to the content of this book. These resources can also be found online at the following URLs:

www.seancrookston.com/publications

www.harleystagner.com/publications

About the Authors

Sean Crookston currently is a data center implementation engineer at TBL Networks, a VMware Enterprise Solutions Provider in Richmond, Virginia. Sean holds certifications from VMware, Cisco, EMC, and Microsoft. Throughout his career, Sean has engineered technology solutions for the healthcare, government, manufacturing, publishing/broadcast, and high-tech industries that streamline business processes and reduce operational expenses. Sean has been awarded the VMware vExpert award in 2010 and 2011.

Harley Stagner is a VMware Certified Design Expert (VCDX #46) and the first VCDX in Virginia. Harley is currently a datacenter design architect at TBL Networks, a VMware Enterprise Solutions Provider in Richmond, Virginia. Harley is focused on vSphere Architecture utilizing the latest datacenter technologies. Harley maintains a blog about these specialties at harleystagner.com. A list of Harley's other publications can be found at www.harleystagner.com/publications.

Acknowledgments

Before we begin this book, we would like to thank the many people who helped us along the way. First, we would like to thank our wives and families for their dedication to this endeavor. Without their patience throughout the writing process, this book would not be possible.

Second, we would like to thank the production and editorial team at VMware Press/Pearson and our technical editors, Russell Pope and Glenn Drawdy, for their dedication to this book.

Third, we would like to thank TBL Networks, Inc., for providing us use of its lab for testing and developing much of the content in this book.

We Want to Hear from You!

As the reader of this book, *you* are our most important critic and commentator. We value your opinion and want to know what we're doing right, what we could do better, what areas you'd like to see us publish in, and any other words of wisdom you're willing to pass our way.

As an associate publisher for Pearson, I welcome your comments. You can email or write me directly to let me know what you did or didn't like about this book—as well as what we can do to make our books better.

Please note that I cannot help you with technical problems related to the topic of this book. We do have a User Services group, however, where I will forward specific technical questions related to the book.

When you write, please be sure to include this book's title and authors as well as your name, email address, and phone number. I will carefully review your comments and share them with the authors and editors who worked on the book.

Email: VMwarePress@vmware.com

Mail: David Dusthimer
        Associate Publisher
        Pearson
        800 East 96th Street
        Indianapolis, IN 46240 USA

Reader Services

Visit our website at www.informit.com/title/9780321820471 and register this book for convenient access to any updates, downloads, or errata that might be available for this book.

Chapter 1

Laying the Groundwork

Planning

Planning is often viewed as a roadblock to innovation. As information technology (IT) practitioners, we often want to bring innovation to our environments quickly. We have seen many deployments where the crucial planning steps are skipped because of the enthusiasm displayed by IT professionals.

Although it might seem like the benefits of the technology are realized sooner, skipping the planning phases of a virtualization project can lead to trouble down the road. You must start with a solid foundation to build upon in the virtual infrastructure so that it meets the needs of today and the scalability of tomorrow. From resource allocation and hardware choice to vSphere configuration, the choices you make during the planning stages will have a significant impact on how effective the virtual infrastructure is at meeting organizational goals.

This chapter is all about laying the foundation for a successful virtualization project. Guidance is given on planning for capacity and performance. Then the chapter moves on to hardware options and the design choices that they can bring. Finally, you explore some common vSphere configuration decisions and how they might affect the infrastructure.

Capacity

As much as users outside of the infrastructure team would like to think that virtual machines are free, they are not. Virtual machines require resources just like physical machines do. The resource requirements for virtual machines must be planned out carefully because most likely they will be utilizing shared resources.

There are two main facets to discuss when capacity planning: performance and capacity. Performance needs for the virtual infrastructure are dictated by the performance needs of the applications residing in the virtual infrastructure in aggregate. Capacity needs for the virtual infrastructure are dictated by the resource usage of the workloads residing in the virtual infrastructure in aggregate. We need to plan how much of a given resource we need (capacity) and how fast that resource should be in relation to a given workload (performance). The workloads in a virtual infrastructure need to reside somewhere, so the next section discusses capacity.

Overview of Planning for Capacity

Server virtualization gives you the flexibility to keep up with changing demands in your day-to-day support of business operations. You can rapidly provision new workloads. You can test new applications. You can provide more resources to an application on demand. You can do all of these things that are not possible in the physical world if you plan for the capacity of the virtual infrastructure to meet these demands and scale appropriately.

When I first decided that I wanted to specialize in virtualization technology, all I wanted to do was play with the technology. The timeline to innovate for my business was no longer than it took me to install the hypervisor. This led to resource scalability problems when the infrastructure grew beyond the initial implementation. The allure of this technology makes it difficult at times to take a step back and plan the infrastructure properly. Whether you are planning for new applications or planning to virtualize existing applications, the first step in standing up any component of a virtual infrastructure should be capacity planning.

New Applications

Planning for new applications is a bit more difficult than planning for existing applications. You must be cognizant of the resource requirements that the application vendor recommends and possibly adjust them to more realistic virtual resource requirements. The following are general recommendations when planning for new applications:

- Always check with the application vendor to see whether they have virtualization recommendations and not just physical application specifications.

- Try to benchmark the application in a test environment before planning for production hardware sizing.

- Check to see whether the application vendor offers a virtual appliance in either the Open Virtualization Appliance (OVA) or Open Virtualization Format (OVF) deployment option. This can cut down on the testing/deployment time considerably.

Virtual machines hosting new applications may be oversized at the onset. Continuously monitor these virtual machines and adjust the resource allocation to be more appropriate over time.

Don't assume that an application cannot be virtualized. Push back on the application vendors if they claim that their application cannot be virtualized. Very few applications cannot be virtualized using today's technology. Having said this, we do not recommend virtualizing an application if the vendor still will not give a written support statement for the particular application in a virtual environment. Hard documentation of application vendors' support should be kept. This might include screen prints, emails, or other correspondence with the application vendor.

Existing Applications

When capacity planning for a virtual infrastructure, look at the four core resources (CPU, disk, RAM, and network). Because virtualization allows flexibility in resource allocation for applications, we typically look at the utilization and not the assignment of the core resources. Let's take a look at the following example. We have a physical system with the following specifications:

- **CPU**—Four total cores, 3,056MHz per core
- **RAM**—4GB
- **Disk**—615GB total capacity
- **Network**—Two 1GbE network interface cards (NICs)

Does this mean that the virtual machine supporting this workload must match these exact specifications? Of course not. One of the reasons that virtualization works so well is that hardware resources are grossly underutilized. So, take a look at the actual utilization of this system to determine its virtual requirements:

- Peak CPU utilization—17%
- Peak RAM utilization—31%
- Disk capacity utilization—19%
- Network utilization—Less than 1%

The adjusted virtual machine specifications, then, are as follows:

- **CPU**—2,079MHz needed (can be satisfied by one vCPU)
- **RAM**—1.24GB of RAM needed (give the virtual machine [VM] 1.5GB of RAM to start)

- **Disk**—116.85GB of disk space needed (consider thin provisioning to grow on demand)

- **Network**—Less than 1% utilization (this will not come close to saturating a 1Gbe link)

Collecting the Data

You can use many methods to collect data on the four core resources. Windows and Linux systems include built-in tools that will collect CPU utilization, RAM utilization, Disk I/O, and Network I/O. The problem with these tools is that out of the box the collection is a manual process that can be very time consuming when you want to get results quickly.

If you are planning a virtual infrastructure of any size beyond a handful of workloads, you will want to automate the collection as much as possible. You can use a tool such as VMware Capacity Planner to collect the necessary data. VMware Capacity Planner is available to authorized VMware partners. If you are a partner, you should have access to this tool. If you are a customer, ask your VMware partner about setting up a VMware capacity planning engagement.

The automated collection of a number of performance and capacity statistics related to virtual infrastructure will help to speed up the planning process. VMware Capacity Planner can be used on Linux and Windows systems and is completely agentless. A service called the data collector runs on the network to gather the statistics. On Windows systems, the data collector utilizes remote Registry and wmi/perfmon to collect the data. On Linux systems, the data collector utilizes Secure Shell (SSH) to collect the data. There are also options in the data collector to make anonymous items such as host names for those businesses that need to do so for security compliance.

Normalizing the Data

In a real-world physical infrastructure, a variety of different server specifications will provide the capacity planning data needed to design the hardware specifications for the virtual infrastructure. This data will need to be normalized across all the data points for it to be meaningful.

For example, you might have a system that is using 95% of its CPU resources. If it is an older system, it may have a total of only 1,500MHz available to it. The 1,425MHz needed is well below the capabilities of a single core in modern processors. So how do you normalize this data? Let's take a look at the following process.

Gather the raw capacity planning data and organize the following items:

- Number of concurrent VMs that will run on the infrastructure
- Average CPU per physical system (MHz)
- Average CPU count per physical system (total cores)
- Average peak CPU utilization per physical system (percentage)
- Average RAM per physical system (MB)
- Average peak RAM utilization per physical system (percentage)

Next, gather the proposed or desired host specification information:

- **CPU**—Sockets per host
- **CPU**—Cores per CPU
- **CPU**—MHz per core
- **RAM**—MB per host

Now that you have the raw data, you can calculate your capacity needs using the following formulas:

- **CPU**

    - Average CPU per physical (MHz) × Average CPU count = Normalized average CPU per physical (MHz)
    - Average peak CPU utilization (percentage) × Normalized average CPU per physical (MHz) = Average peak CPU utilization (MHz)
    - Number of concurrent VMs × Average peak CPU utilization (MHz) = Total peak CPU utilization (MHz)

CPU Example:

3,103MHz × 4 = 12,412MHz

12,412MHz × 16.00% = 1,985.92MHz

100 × 1,985.92MHz = 198,592MHz

198,592MHz is what will be required for this virtual infrastructure.

- **RAM**
  - Average RAM per physical (MB) × Average peak RAM utilization (percentage) = Average peak RAM utilization (MB)
  - Number of concurrent VMs × Average peak RAM utilization (MB) = Total peak RAM utilization (MB)

NOTE

Depending on the operating systems and applications running on a particular host, the Transparent Page Sharing (TPS) mechanism of vSphere can be used to share memory pages among virtual machines. In homogeneous operating system environments, we typically estimate a 33% RAM benefit from TPS.

RAM Example:

4,363MB × 55.00% = 2399.65MB

100 × 2399.65MB = 239,965MB

239,965MB is what will be required for this virtual infrastructure.

- **Host CPU specifications:**
  - CPU sockets per host × Cores per CPU = Cores per host
  - MHz per core × Cores per host = MHz per host
  - Maximum CPU utilization allowed per host (percentage) × MHz per host = CPU available per host

Host CPU Specification Example:

2 × 10 = 20

2,400MHz × 20 = 48,000MHz

80% × 48,000MHz = 38,400MHz

38,400MHz is available per host.

- **Host RAM specifications:**

  - RAM per host (MB) × Maximum RAM utilization allowed per host (percentage) = RAM available per host

---

Host RAM Specification Example:

131,072MB × 80% = 104,857.6MB

104,857.6MB is available per host.

NOTE

We generally recommend leaving 20% of host resources free for any overhead and spikes that may occur. An example of this overhead might be a VMware HA failover event before DRS balances the load.

- **Number of hosts per CPU requirements:**

  - Total peak CPU utilization (MHz) / CPU (MHZ) available per host = Number of hosts required per CPU requirements (round up)

  - Number of hosts required per CPU requirements + 1 = Number of hosts required per CPU requirements for N+1 redundancy

---

Number of Hosts per CPU Requirements Example:

198,592MHz / 38,400MHz = 5.171666667 = 6 rounded up

6 + 1 = 7

Seven hosts are required for N+1 redundancy from a CPU perspective.

- **Number of hosts per RAM requirements:**

  - Total peak RAM utilization (MB) / RAM (MB) available per host = Number of hosts required per RAM requirements (round up)

  - Number of hosts required per RAM requirements + 1 = Number of hosts required per RAM requirements for N+1 redundancy

---

Number of Hosts per RAM Requirement Example:

239,965MB / 104,857.6MB = 2.288484573 = 3 rounded up

3 + 1 = 4

Four hosts are required for N+1 redundancy from a RAM perspective.

The number of hosts needed will be the worst-case scenario.

Increased Host per RAM Requirement Example:

Seven hosts are required for N+1 redundancy from a CPU perspective.

Four hosts are required for N+1 redundancy from a RAM perspective.

Seven hosts are required for N+1 redundancy for the virtual infrastructure.

NOTE

Most environments that you will encounter are memory bound and not CPU bound. The previous example was used to show that some workloads can also be CPU bound. Part of the benefit of capacity planning is that you can uncover these details and make appropriate hardware decisions based on them.

Network Capacity Planning

Generally speaking, very few workloads would even saturate a 1GbE connection, much less a 10GbE connection. So, this section discusses network capacity planning from a port count perspective. How many ports will the virtualization solution need? To discuss this in detail, you must first understand three different virtual infrastructure architectures: traditional 1GbE, converged rackmount, and converged blade.

Traditional 1GbE Architecture

Figure 1.1 depicts a traditional 1GbE virtual infrastructure architecture. This architecture is, perhaps, the easiest to understand because it has been around the longest. A typical vSphere host will have eight to ten 1GbE ports connecting to upstream switches depending on the storage architecture. This is because it is a generally accepted best practice to separate different types of network traffic on a vSphere host. For example, it is not uncommon to separate the traffic as shown in Figure 1.2.

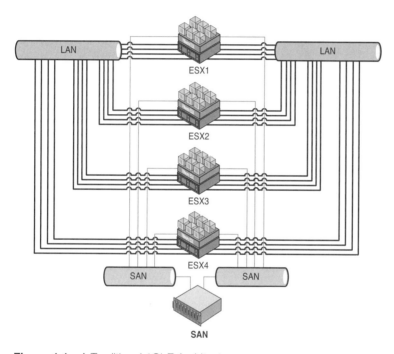

Figure 1.1 A Traditional 1GbE Architecture

- **Management**—VMkernel (two NICs)

- **vMotion**—VMkernel (two NICs)

- **Fault tolerance**—VMkernel (two NICs)

- **Storage**—VMkernel (two NICs)

- **VM traffic**—Virtual machine network (two NICs)

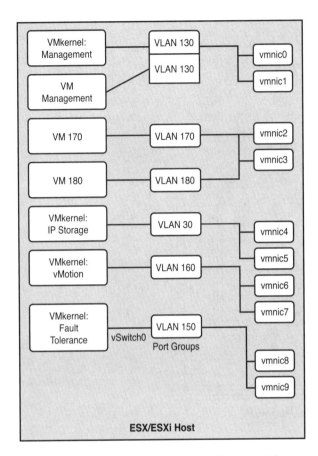

Figure 1.2   Port Group Layout for Traditional Architecture

As this infrastructure is scaled, the number of cables and ports required can become problematic. In Figure 1.2's traffic separation example, there are ten ports per host spread across multiple switches for connectivity. This means that a single 24-port switch will just barely handle the port count of half the NIC ports on four vSphere hosts. As more hosts are added, there are other options that offer greater scalability.

Converged Rackmount Architecture

Figure 1.3 depicts a converged rackmount architecture. This architecture consolidates the traditional 1GbE connectivity into a 10GbE infrastructure by connecting to a Fibre Channel over Ethernet (FCoE) or straight 10GbE switch. This allows more bandwidth and cuts down on the port count required as you scale this infrastructure. The port count is much more manageable in this architecture. The cable and port count still scales linearly with the hosts. This means that port count can still be an issue in larger environments. However, you do have more room for growth before you need to consider purchasing more switches.

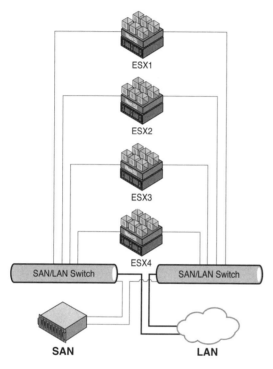

Figure 1.3   Converged Rackmount Architecture

Both the converged rackmount architecture and the converged blade architecture typically have only two NIC ports to work with on each vSphere host. Generally, there will be one vSwitch with the traffic types separated by port group, as depicted in Figure 1.4

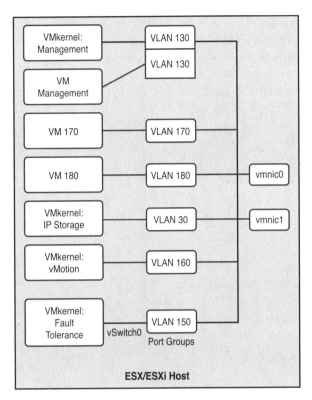

Figure 1.4 Port Group Layout for Converged Rackmount and Converged Blade Architectures

Converged Blade Architecture

Figure 1.5 is an example of a converged blade architecture using the Cisco Unified Computing System (UCS) blade system. Note that the bandwidth and port count calculations from a network perspective happen at the UCS 6100 series fabric interconnects (Blade Mgmt in the diagram). Think of them as a network and storage aggregation layer. Do you need 20Gb of bandwidth for your blade servers downstream from the 6100 series? No problem; just add two 10Gb uplinks to each 6100 series fabric interconnect. Do you need 40Gb? Just add four 10Gb uplinks, and so on. In this architecture, you are not as concerned with bringing the network bandwidth calculation and port count all the way to the blade servers themselves. Sure, you need some cabling for connectivity to the 6100 series fabric interconnects, but it is dramatically reduced because you can share bandwidth among the blade servers. This architecture gives you predictable performance and incremental network scalability that does not rely on a linear relationship to the number of vSphere hosts in a given infrastructure.

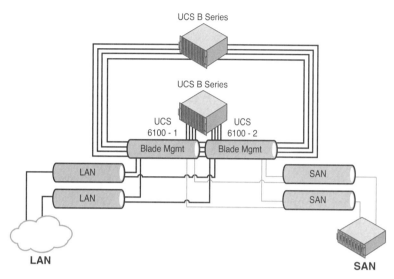

Figure 1.5   Converged Blade Architecture

Although a deep design discussion of these architectures is beyond the scope of this book, it is important to have some familiarity with them to properly plan for a given architecture. It is much easier to manage an infrastructure if it is properly planned for in the beginning. The main takeaway when planning for network capacity is as follows:

- Determine your architecture.

- Determine your bandwidth needs.

- Determine your isolation needs.

- Determine your port count.

Performance

In almost all cases, we recommend planning for performance, then capacity. This is especially true from a storage perspective. We have been called into many environments that were experiencing performance problems due to undersized resources. If you only consider capacity, the infrastructure may perform well at first. However, as more workloads are added, performance decreases over time.

Capacity can be cheap from a storage perspective. You can now deploy drives in a storage array that are 3TB in size; however, these drives are typically slow. If only a few are used to provide the capacity needed, then the entire environment may suffer from performance issues because resources are being shared in a virtual infrastructure. The rule of thumb here is to plan for performance first, then make up the capacity if needed.

Overview of Planning for Performance

As a data center consultant, I have the privilege of working with many different clients and many types of infrastructures. I often run into hesitation or outright refusal to virtualize *mission-critical* applications. Mission critical can mean something different to different businesses. Whatever the meaning, there is usually some kind of database involved. This could be SQL, Oracle, Exchange, and so forth. Every single time I run into objections, there is some concern over performance. Some of the concerns and questions that I still get today include: "I heard you can't virtualize SQL because it is too heavy of a workload."; "I don't want to subject my mission-critical application to any performance degradation."; "Doesn't virtualization introduce overhead?"

The overhead from virtualization has been negligible for almost all workloads since Virtual Infrastructure 3, and it just keeps getting more negligible. For example, VMware recently did a lab test with EMC and achieved 1,000,000 I/O operations per second from a single vSphere 5 host and 300,000 I/O operations per second from a single virtual machine. Considering that the average total I/O per second in the small to medium enterprise space that I deal with is approximately 5,000–15,000 I/O per second, there is plenty of performance to spare.

We usually explain that a poorly designed foundation will suffer performance problems whether physical or virtual. You cannot simply plan for capacity only and expect to have a solid infrastructure. You must plan for performance as well.

Planning for Storage Performance

Servers that have come out within the last couple of years are reasonably powerful enough to not worry so much about the specific feeds and speeds of the CPU and memory. As long as you plan for enough CPU and memory capacity, performance will be there. The same cannot be said of storage.

This section discusses planning for storage performance specifically because it is the most critical piece of the virtual infrastructure. Storage is also where poor planning can have the most negative impact on performance.

Although you could spend hours looking into tweaking things like Host Bus Adapter (HBA) parameters and advanced storage array parameters, this section focuses on practical advice for sizing an infrastructure appropriately for disk I/O operations per second (IOPS) or megabytes per second (MBps). The more advanced tweaking is typically done under the guidance of your particular storage manufacturer.

The guidance here is for worst-case scenario performance sizing. There are many factors to consider when choosing a storage array, including the amount of cache, parity handling, and so on. To have a consistent general discussion on planning for storage performance, we stick to what the disks themselves are capable of.

When planning for storage performance, you look at two general metrics: IOPS and MBps. IOPS is measuring the raw number of I/O requests that can be handled by the storage array per second. Usually IOPS is concerned more with the back-end disk subsystem as the spindles are what provide this performance metric. MBps is more of a bandwidth measurement. How much data can we push to the back-end disk subsystem before it becomes saturated? Or, how much data is required to be pushed to the back-end disks by the workload?

The methodology that you will use when planning for storage performance involves gathering three key metrics:

- IOPS (sometimes referred to as I/O transfers per second)

- Read rate in KBps (converted to MBps)

- Write rate in KBps (converted to MBps)

The easiest way to collect this data is to utilize VMware Capacity Planner through VMware or a participating VMware partner because it collects statistics on the entire infrastructure that you are targeting for virtualization. These statistics can also be found by utilizing tools within the operating systems of the individual virtual machines or by using other third-party tools. Once you have gathered the data that you need from all your virtualization targets, you must calculate your storage needs from a performance perspective. Conservatively speaking, the IOPS values for different disks are as follows:

- 7200 RPM SATA or NL-SAS: 90 IOPS

- 15K RPM Fibre Channel (FC) or Serial Attached SCSI (SAS): 180 IOPS

- SSD: 2500

Knowing this, you can calculate the number of disks you need by the type of disks that you choose. For example, suppose you have an IOPS requirement of 15,000 IOPS for your entire workload. To keep it simple for now, let's do a calculation based on using all RAID 5. RAID 5 has a 4X write penalty. This is where our read rate and write rate come in. Let's look at the data that you have collected:

- 15,000 IOPS

- 340,000KBps read rate

- 100,000KBps write rate
- Using 15K SAS disks, the disk count calculation for RAID 5 is

  ((Read% + (4 × Write%)) × (IOPS required)) / IOPS per disk = Disk count

- 340,000KBps + 100,000KBps = 440,000 KBps
- 340,000KBps / 440,000KBps = ~77.27% Read percentage
- 100,000KBps / 440,000KBps = ~22.72% Write percentage

  ((77.27% + (4 × 22.72%)) × (15,000)) / 180 = 140.125

  Rounded up, we will need approximately 141 disks for the workload using RAID 5.

Let's do that same calculation for RAID 1, which has only a 2X write penalty.

RAID 1

((77.27% + (2 × 22.72%)) × (15,000)) / 180 = 102.258

Rounded up, we will need approximately 103 disks for the workload using RAID 1.

What if we use SSDs?

SSD

((77.27% + (4 × 22.72%)) × (15,000)) / 2500 = 10.089

Rounded up, we will need approximately 11 disks for the workload using RAID 5.

((77.27% + (2 × 22.72%)) × (15,000)) / 2500 = 7.3626

Rounded up, we will need approximately 8 disks for the workload using RAID 1.

That's quite a difference from the SAS 15K disks! Unfortunately, from a capacity perspective, SSDs do not make sense. Their cost per gigabyte is way too high. Thankfully, there are storage technologies out there that address the need to balance performance and capacity.

Two technologies that have emerged in recent years help the performance/capacity storage proposition:

- Virtual Storage Pools
- Sub-LUN Storage Tiering

To fully understand how these technologies help us today, let's review the traditional approach to configuring enterprise storage arrays. Let's define a couple of terms first:

- **RAID Group**—A group of physical disks that are configured into a specific RAID level

- **Logical Unit Number (LUN)**—A logical unit of storage that is presented to the host

Figure 1.6 shows an example of a traditional storage layout.

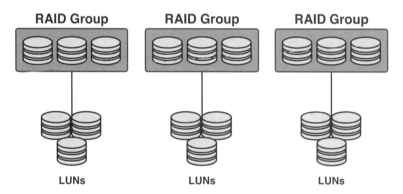

Figure 1.6 Traditional Storage Layout

Traditionally, enterprise storage arrays have been configured with these general steps:

1. An IOPS amount is determined.

2. A number of disks are determined to fulfill that IOPS requirement.

3. Those disks are configured into one or more RAID groups.

4. Those RAID groups are configured into one or more LUN(s).

5. Those LUNs are presented to the hosts to be used for storage.

This is a very straightforward configuration and performance is well understood. There is, however, very little room for flexibility in this architecture. Let's look at our 15,000 IOPS workload again.

It required approximately 141 15K SAS disks in a RAID-5 configuration, 103 15K SAS disks in a RAID-1 configuration, or 11 SSD disks in a RAID-5 configuration. In a traditional storage architecture, the disks must generally be the same speed and capacity. So, to provide the IOPS for the workload, you may end up with a great deal of wasted capacity because 141 15K SAS disks are required for a RAID-5 configuration. On the other hand, you would cut your capacity in half if you were to use a RAID-1 configuration and only use 38 fewer disks. You only need 11 SSD disks in a RAID-5 configuration, but those 11 disks are not likely to come close to the capacity needs of the particular workload.

This architecture is not the most efficient use of storage resources because you are locked in to rigid RAID groups. This is where Virtual Storage Pools and Sub-LUN Tiering can help. They work together to make a much more flexible solution.

Virtual Storage Pools can be made up of many different speeds and capacities of disks. The underlying RAID level of the storage pool is at a level that is lower than the Virtual Storage Pool. There is just a pool of storage that can be presented as LUNs to a host. Sub-LUN Tiering works to move blocks of storage (at the sub-LUN level) to the most appropriate performance tier for the workload. This means that portions of a virtual machine that are provisioned in a Sub-LUN Tiering–enabled Virtual Storage Pool can exist on SSDs while other portions exist on lower-performing disks. This allows you to provide the majority of the IOPS needed with only a few SSD disks while the other tiers of storage make up the capacity needed.

Every vendor's implementation of this architecture is a little different. This is the principle behind Sub-LUN Tiering at a high level. This architecture provides greater flexibility and easier storage management while utilizing the purchased storage assets more efficiently. Figure 1.7 shows an example of an auto-tiering storage layout.

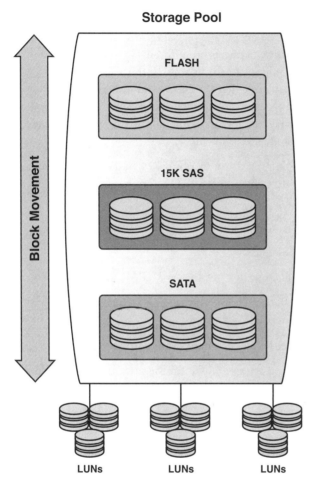

Figure 1.7 Auto-tiering Storage Layout

Management

Management for the virtual infrastructure is just as important as the deployment of
the virtual infrastructure. Although it is important to lay a solid design foundation, an
improperly managed infrastructure can undermine all of the work that was accomplished
in the beginning to lay that solid foundation. Managing the virtual infrastructure is
covered in more detail in Chapter 4, "Managing the Environment." For now, let's discuss
some things that you should be thinking about when planning for the management of the
virtual infrastructure.

Overview of Planning for Management

You might have picked up on the fact that we encourage planning throughout the virtual infrastructure life cycle. Managing the infrastructure is no different. Before you deploy the first host server, you should have a plan in place for how the infrastructure will be managed. Management considerations may even affect some of your design decisions. So how do you go about planning for management? Experience has shown that asking the right questions helps to solidify a management plan. Some of the questions that can uncover what needs to be considered include the following:

- Who will be responsible for managing the firmware? Software updates for the underlying infrastructure hardware and virtualization layer? Operating system layer and Application layer?

- How often should updates be deployed?

- How will updates be tested and validated?

- What monitoring mechanisms will be put in place (SNMP, CIM, and so on)?

- Who is responsible for resource management, deploying new virtual machines, and deciding when more resources are needed?

- What tools will be used to automate the management of the infrastructure?

- Do management tools offer role-based access control for the infrastructure if security compliance regulations are required?

These are an example of the types of questions that should be asked when planning for management. Gather the correct people and discuss these questions. This will lead you down the correct path toward a well-managed infrastructure and possibly cause you to consider new management approaches.

Designing

Designing a virtual infrastructure is a multidisciplinary effort. You must gather input from many different sources and create a holistic design from that data. Design is about more than deciding on and configuring hardware resources. The design should take into account multiple facets of the infrastructure, including capacity, performance, security, implementation, management, business continuity, and disaster recovery. This book is not focused entirely on the design process. However, a high-level discussion of the design process is discussed here for context.

Design Process Overview

The design process is an ongoing exercise that begins with infrastructure planning and continues with managing and maintaining the infrastructure. The initial design process is discussed here. Generally speaking, you should follow the listed design workflow, adjusting it to suit your specific needs.

1. Gather requirements, constraints, and assumptions for the design from the appropriate stakeholders.

2. Perform analysis that may include capacity planning to help determine the resources that will be required for the design.

3. Produce design documentation that minimally includes a logical and physical architecture, implementation and configuration procedures, operational verification procedures, and a design blueprint that includes diagrams for the design.

4. When creating the design and documentation, incorporate the facets of capacity, performance, security, implementation, management, business continuity, and disaster recovery into the overall solution.

5. Be sure to note design considerations, decisions, justifications for those decisions, and the impact of those decisions when creating the design documentation.

6. Make sure all stakeholders sign off on the design documentation and agree on a deviation procedure before implementing the design.

7. Review the design with the stakeholders and the implementation team to ensure that the design is as complete as possible. Things will be missed. However, this can be mitigated with proper review of the design.

8. Review any design expansion considerations, such as company mergers and acquisitions. How will capacity/feature addition be handled in the organization?

This is a general overview of the design process. It is very important that everyone agrees on the direction of the design moving forward. After the initial design and implementation, the infrastructure must be managed on an ongoing basis and design considerations must be continually reviewed to ensure that they still make sense for the changing environment. Managing, operating, and optimizing the virtual infrastructure is what the rest of the chapters in this book focus on.

Design Decisions

Throughout the design process, you will make many decisions. The key to any solid decision is understanding the impact of that decision and clearly communicating the justification for that decision. Keep this in mind for your specific environment. The following sections outline some common decisions that you may encounter.

Choosing Hardware

From a resource perspective, the hardware chosen will be decided upon by the capacity planning. However, you may also consider management in the decision. You should explore the different infrastructures (traditional 1GbE, converged rackmount, and converged blade) before making any hardware decisions. Look at the pros and cons of each infrastructure type. At a high level, Table 1.1 shows some discussion points that can help your decision.

Table 1.1   Pros and Cons of Each Infrastructure Type

Infrastructure Type	Pro	Con
Traditional 1GbE	The infrastructure is well understood	This infrastructure does not scale well beyond a few host servers from a port count perspective
Converged rackmount	The infrastructure scales much better than traditional 1GbE	Port count scalability is still directly proportional to the number of host servers
Converged blade	Port count is determined more appropriately by true bandwidth needs	More up-front investment may be required to gain scalability benefits

From a storage perspective, you should look at a unified storage solution that is capable of supporting many protocols (FC, iSCSI, NFS, and CIFS) and may take advantage of different drive sizes and types. Flexibility and efficiency are the keys here. For example, we do not virtualize file servers for many of our clients. Instead, we consolidate the file serving onto the storage array itself. This avoids having to deal with managing file server operating systems such as Windows and allows the infrastructure to scale much more seamlessly from a file serving perspective.

Many hardware choices are available. The key is choosing hardware that covers the majority of your infrastructure needs while simplifying the deployment. The fewer moving pieces in the infrastructure, the better off you will be.

Choosing Configuration

You must make many configuration choices when deploying a vSphere architecture. As with any technology, there are some features that should generally be used in any circumstance, some features that might be nice to have but have some impact on your particular environment, and some features that should be used only in certain circumstances. This section does not propose every circumstance and feature. It does cover some sensible decisions and approaches when it comes to vSphere configuration.

This section first discusses the features that have been serving as the foundation of a solid virtual infrastructure for many years, and then goes on to discuss some newer features that vSphere 5 brings to the table. The foundation features that have been used for years are High Availability (HA), vMotion, and Distributed Resource Scheduler (DRS). You should absolutely be using these features in your design if they are available.

High Availability

vSphere HA is used for unplanned downtime. vSphere HA will automatically restart virtual machines that are part of the same HA/DRS cluster if there is a hardware failure of one of the hosts within the cluster. There are some configuration decisions to make when vSphere HA is deployed beyond the initial setup.

Admission Control Policy   Generally, HA admission control should be enabled. Then, the question becomes which admission control policy should be used. Plenty of resources are available that lay out the pros and cons of the different admission control policies. As a refresher, the following admission control policies are available:

- **Host Failures Cluster Tolerates (slot-based)**—This policy enables you to set how many host failures the cluster can tolerate. To determine how much capacity is reserved for failover "slots," defined by worst-case "per-VM" reservations of CPU and memory, HA slots are used. HA slots are a relatively complex mechanism. Due to this complexity, we recommend exploring the other admission control policies as they focus on flexibility and simplicity.

- **Percentage of Cluster Resources Reserved as Failover Spare Capacity (percentage-based)**—This policy enables you to set a certain percentage of both CPU and memory as failover capacity. The percentage of resources left for failover is determined by actual per-VM reservations so it is more flexible than the slot-based admission control policy.

- **Specify Failover Hosts**—This policy is pretty straightforward. You specify one or more hosts to be designated failover hosts. When a failover occurs, the designated failover hosts will attempt to be used. These designated failover hosts cannot be used as resources in the cluster until there is an actual failover event.

We recommend using the Percentage of Cluster Resources Reserved as Failover Spare Capacity (percentage-based) admission control policy. We realize that we cannot cover every possible environment out there. This policy offers the greatest flexibility while covering the widest variety of use cases in our experience.

So, given that the percentage-based admission control policy will be used in the infrastructure, let's discuss how that should be configured given the following assumptions:

- A cluster of balanced host servers is used from a resource perspective (identical CPU and RAM)

- N+1 redundancy is required

NOTE

We recommend that you should always utilize identical hosts in a cluster whenever possible. The more uniform the configurations, the better (CPU and RAM as well as logical configuration).

Let's say that you have five host servers. Each server has the following resources:

- **CPU**—48GHz

- **RAM**—128GB

You want to provide the equivalent of one host worth of resources as failover capacity because N+1 redundancy is a requirement. You arrive at this percentage with a very simple formula:

(Number of hosts needed for redundancy / Number of hosts) × 100 = Percentage reserved

Using the previous scenario, you would calculate the percentage as follows:

(1/5) × 100

.20 × 100 = 20

You should use 20% as the amount of resources reserved.

You use the following formulas to determine the amount of resources in the cluster for virtual machines plus overhead:

CPU

CPU per host × Number of hosts = Total CPU capacity per cluster

Total CPU capacity per cluster × CPU percentage reserved = CPU capacity reserved for failover

Total CPU capacity per cluster × CPU capacity reserved for failover = CPU capacity reserved for the workload

---

RAM

RAM per host × Number of hosts = Total RAM capacity per cluster

Total RAM capacity per cluster × RAM percentage reserved = RAM capacity reserved for failover

Total RAM capacity per cluster × RAM capacity reserved for failover = RAM capacity reserved for the workload

---

Going back to the previous scenario, you arrive at the following usable capacity in the cluster for virtual machines plus overhead:

CPU

48GHz × 5 = 240GHz

240GHz × 20% = 48GHz

240GHz - 48GHz = 192GHz

192GHz of CPU resource is available to the cluster.

RAM

128GB × 5 = 640GB

640GB × 20% = 128GB

640GB - 128GB = 512GB

512GB of RAM resource is available to the cluster.

VM Monitoring   There are a few choices in the VM Monitoring HA section:

- Leave VM Monitoring Disabled
- Enable VM Monitoring Only
- Enable VM and Application Monitoring

We recommend to at least enable VM Monitoring because it adds an extra layer of failure detection beyond just an ESXi host failure. If you are going to use VM Monitoring, you should keep a few things in mind about how it functions:

- VMware Tools is required to use VM Monitoring on a virtual machine.
- VM Monitoring works by sending a VMware Tools heartbeat to the HA agent on a host.
- If this VMware Tools heartbeat is not received in a specific amount of time, the virtual machine will be restarted.
- To avoid false-positives after no heartbeats are received, disk and network activity is also monitored.
- A virtual machine will restart if the following conditions are met:
    - No VMware Tools heartbeat is received.
    - There is no network activity over a certain interval (120 seconds by default).
    - There is no storage activity over a certain interval (120 seconds by default).
- Default detection intervals and thresholds can be customized to your infrastructure needs.
- When a VM Monitoring–related failover occurs, a screenshot of the VM at the time of failure is automatically taken and stored in the VM directory on the datastore.

Application Monitoring utilizes an application programming interface (API) that will allow developers to write applications or scripts that leverage the API. This may help to restart a virtual machine in the event of an application failure if that application is written to take advantage of the Application Monitoring API. If you can take advantage of this feature in your environment, then enable it. It adds yet another layer of resiliency to your infrastructure.

Datastore Heartbeating   Datastore heartbeating is an extra mechanism that vSphere HA uses to determine whether a host has truly failed or it is isolated/partitioned. If it is determined that a host has been isolated, HA relies on datastore heartbeats to determine whether a host has truly failed. The following are the important points to remember about datastore heartbeating:

■ Datastore heartbeats utilize a file named host-<number>-hb on the chosen datastores to determine whether the datastores are still "alive."

■ By default, two datastores are chosen for heartbeating.

■ vCenter uses an algorithm to select datastores that are available to all the hosts in a cluster.

■ You have the option to choose the datastores yourself, but it is not generally recommended because it introduces human error to the process.

■ A host is determined to be in a failed state when it is isolated and there are no datastore heartbeats.

NOTE

Converged Networking, where storage and data are traveling over the same NIC or Converged Network Adapter (CNA), may lessen the advantages of datastore heartbeating because a NIC or CNA failure can cause datastore heartbeats to fail as well. When in doubt, it is best to consult the hardware vendors for best practices regarding datastore heartbeating. As of this writing, the following process is used for disabling datastore heartbeating:

1. Choose the Select Only from My Preferred Datastores option in Datastore Heartbeating and do not select any datastores.

2. Suppress the vCenter warning message, "The number of vSphere HA heartbeat datastores for this host is 0, which is less than required: 2," by using the advanced setting das.ignoreInsufficientHbDatastore and setting its value to True.

---

vMotion

vMotion allows a live migration of a virtual machine to occur between hosts. There are few configuration choices when setting up vMotion. Typically either a vmkernel port is using vMotion or it is not. However, there are some considerations when using vMotion that we'll review here. First, some general recommendations that we always make:

■ Isolate vMotion traffic on separate NICs whenever possible.

■ If dedicated NICs cannot be used for vMotion, then consider an active/standby configuration with vMotion and management traffic, as shown in Figure 1.8.

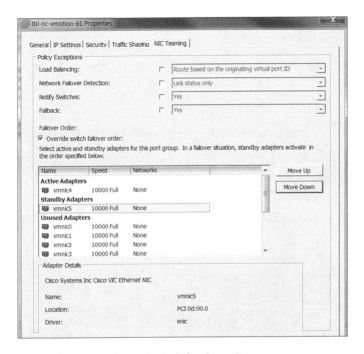

Figure 1.8 Active/Standby NIC Configuration

vMotion traffic is now capable of saturating a 10Gb link. In larger environments, consider utilizing vSphere Network I/O Control (NIOC) or some other bandwidth management/ Quality of Service (QoS) mechanism to reduce the priority of vMotion traffic on the network.

At the time of this writing, four simultaneous vMotion migrations are allowed on 1GbE links and eight simultaneous vMotion migrations are allowed on 10GbE links. Consider using 10GbE links for vMotion to increase scalability.

vSphere 5 introduced multi-NIC vMotion capability that will use multiple NICs in parallel for a vMotion. This works even when a single VM is being migrated using vMotion. Consider setting up multi-NIC vMotion to further increase vMotion scalability.

Setting Up Multi-NIC vMotion

Setting up multi-NIC vMotion is a relatively straightforward process. Follow these steps:

1. Create a VMkernel port and select the Enable vMotion option.

2. Configure one NIC for this VMkernel port as active under Failover Order and all other NICs that will participate in vMotion as standby.

3. Create another VMkernel port and select the Enable vMotion option.

4. Configure a different NIC for this VMkernel port as active under Failover Order and all other NICs that will participate in vMotion as standby.

Repeat this process for all the NICs that you would like to use for multi-NIC vMotion. You can use a total of sixteen 1GbE and four 10GbE adapters for multi-NIC vMotion configurations. Figure 1.9 shows a sample configuration for a two-NIC vMotion VMkernel port.

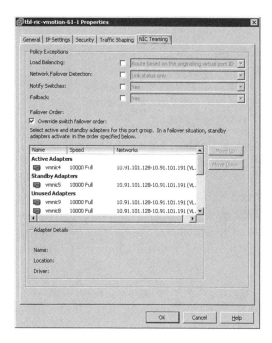

Figure 1.9   Configuration for a Two-NIC vMotion VMkernel Port

10Gb, Virtual Hardware Adapters, and Design Impact

The addition of multi-NIC vMotion and the fact that a single vMotion can use up to 8Gb worth of bandwidth is a welcome addition for vMotion scalability. As with any technology feature, you must think about how it impacts the overall design.

If you are using a two-port 10Gb converged infrastructure on your host servers, you might need to ensure that vMotion traffic does not restrict more important traffic types, such as VM traffic. The vSphere method to control different types of traffic traversing the same NIC is Network IO Control (NIOC) used on a distributed vSwitch. This feature enables you to assign shares to network resources. In times of contention, these shares will determine how much bandwidth certain traffic types (vMotion, iSCSI, FT, VM, and so on) will receive. If you do not have access to the vSphere-distributed vSwitch or cannot use it because of some design consideration, there are hardware approaches to shaping the bandwidth.

Some vendors have specialized 10Gb NICs that enable you to divide the NIC into a number of virtual NICs that the ESXi host can see. For example, if you divide the NIC into ten virtual NICs, the ESXi server will see ten NICs available to assign to ESXi host networking. Depending on the vendor, you might be able to implement either traffic policing or QoS shaping to each virtual NIC. A complete discussion about different networking QoS methods is beyond the scope of this text. Following is an overview of traffic policing and QoS shaping.

Traffic policing is a method used to control the amount of bandwidth that a certain traffic type gets. For example, if using virtual hardware NICs, you could assign a 2Gb bandwidth to the virtual NICs that are assigned to vMotion traffic. vMotion could not use any bandwidth beyond the 2Gb on that particular set of NICs due to the policing.

QoS shaping enables you to assign a priority to different traffic types. For example, vMotion traffic may receive a lower priority than VM traffic. This is an important architectural distinction when comparing QoS shaping with traffic policing. When traffic policing is used, the vMotion traffic could never use any bandwidth beyond what was assigned to it. When QoS shaping is used, vMotion traffic could use as much bandwidth (up to 8Gb per vMotion) as is available if it did not interfere with higher priority traffic. If it were going to interfere, the priority would kick in and give the higher priority traffic the "right of way." QoS shaping is a more flexible solution because it allows full use of the bandwidth unless there is contention.

The decision to use QoS shaping or traffic policing also has an impact on how vMotion will function in the infrastructure. Depending on the vendor implementation, traffic policing may cause ESXi to see a NIC speed that is equal to whatever the bandwidth is policed at. For example, if a particular virtual hardware NIC was set to 2Gb worth of bandwidth, ESXi may only see a 2Gb-capable NIC. If this NIC is used for vMotion, then only four simultaneous vMotions would be allowed because ESXi does not see a 10Gb NIC. With QoS shaping, eight simultaneous vMotions would be allowed because ESXi would see a 10Gb NIC.

DRS

There is no doubt that we recommend turning on DRS if it is available. Once enabled, DRS has three automation levels:

- **Manual**—Migration recommendations suggested by vCenter

- **Partially Automated**—Automatic VM placement with migration recommendations from vCenter

■ **Fully Automated**—Automatic VM placement and automatic VM migration to optimize resource usage

Unless an application specifically states that DRS is not supported, we recommend using the Fully Automated DRS automation level. If DRS is set to Fully Automated, you do not have to manage resource balancing as much and you can use Maintenance mode to automatically migrate virtual machines to other hosts within the cluster. DRS has been around long enough in VMware infrastructures that it should be fully trusted when everything is set up properly. As with any feature, it should be tested to ensure proper functionality before placing the resources into production and when changed afterward.

Affinity/Anti-Affinity VM to VM DRS Rules   Affinity rules keep virtual machines together on the same host when making DRS suggestions. Anti-affinity rules keep virtual machines separated on different hosts. We recommend that they be used when necessary to eliminate risk or management overhead. Too many rules can lead to imbalanced clusters due to limited DRS recommendation options and more management overhead. The following are some examples of when affinity/anti-affinity rules should be used:

■ Use anti-affinity rules when you have applications that need to be separated for added resiliency or security reasons (for example, Active Directory domain controllers).

■ Use affinity rules to keep network traffic between application servers on the virtual switch without the need to travel to upstream switches (for example, database and Web server pair).

Affinity/Anti-Affinity VM to Host Rules   VM to Host affinity and anti-affinity rules were introduced in vSphere 4.1. These rules control which hosts certain virtual machines can and cannot be run on in a DRS cluster. A VM to Host rule requires three components:

■ **VM group**—Group of selected VMs

■ **Host group**—Group of selected hosts

■ **A rule**—Either affinity to host group or anti-affinity to host group

When creating the rule, there are four possibilities:

■ Must run on a certain host group

■ Must not run on a certain host group

■ Should run on a certain host group

■ Should not run on a certain host group

These "must" rules will never be violated and rule information is provided to HA. That means that if a "must" rule is used, vSphere HA will only use the selected hosts that a VM is allowed to run on as failover hosts. A "should" rule is enforced on a "best-effort" basis and DRS will only violate these rules if absolutely necessary. Some examples of VM to Host DRS rules are as follows:

- VM Group (DB VMs) must run on host group (DB Hosts)

- VM Group (DB VMs) must not run on host group (Non-DB Hosts)

- VM Group (DB VMs) should run on host group (DB Hosts)

- VM Group (DB VMs) should not run on host group (Non-DB Hosts)

There are many use cases for VM to Host affinity/anti-affinity rules. As with the VM to VM affinity/anti-affinity rules, we recommend using them only when absolutely necessary. These rules can make cluster troubleshooting and failover calculations more difficult. In our experience, the most compelling reason to use a VM to Host affinity or anti-affinity rule is to control VM mobility for applications that might not be licensed for every host server while still allowing other VMs to run on the hosts in question. These rules can also be used to ensure that vCenter runs on only a couple of hosts in a larger cluster so that it is easier to find in the event of an outage. The only alternative before these rules was to run a separate cluster for licensing purposes. That is no longer the case.

> **NOTE**
>
> If you want to maintain true N+1 redundancy when using VM to Host affinity rules, then you should calculate the N+1 redundancy for each host group instead of just on the cluster as a whole.

Storage DRS

Storage DRS is one of the most exciting new features of vSphere 5. Because it has not been around that long, this section does not make specific recommendations regarding Storage DRS. Instead, this section discusses some of the benefits that Storage DRS offers and makes some high-level recommendations on how to begin utilizing Storage DRS in your infrastructure. Storage DRS brings three general capabilities:

- Space utilization–based load balancing

- I/O latency–based load balancing

- Anti-affinity rules for virtual disks

Storage DRS uses a concept called a datastore cluster to aggregate the storage in a vSphere 5 cluster. A datastore cluster is a collection of datastores (either Network File System [NFS] or Virtual Machine File System [VMFS] but not both) that storage DRS can act upon. Storage DRS has two automation levels:

- **No Automation (Manual Mode)**—Initial placement and migration recommendations are displayed. They will not run until you manually apply the recommendation.

- **Fully Automated**—Initial placement and migration recommendations are run automatically.

Space Utilization Load Balancing   This feature lets you set a threshold for disk space usage on a datastore. When the space usage on a datastore exceeds that threshold, Storage DRS can generate recommendations or take an automated Storage vMotion action to balance the space utilization across the datastore cluster.

This feature reduces the administrative overhead involved with deploying virtual machines by making initial placement recommendations based on space utilization within the datastore cluster. Space utilization load balancing also helps to reduce the administrative burden of moving VMs around when space becomes low on certain datastores as this can be done automatically through Storage DRS.

I/O Latency Load Balancing   This feature lets you set a threshold for disk I/O latency. When the I/O latency on a datastore exceeds that threshold, Storage DRS can generate recommendations or take an automated Storage vMotion action to balance the I/O latency across the datastore cluster.

This feature also reduces the administrative overhead involved with deploying virtual machines. However, I/O latency load balancing tackles placement from an I/O load perspective. Instead of making I/O calculations every time you want to deploy a new VM, let Storage DRS make the decision for you. Like space utilization load balancing, I/O latency load balancing can also be used to make ongoing load balancing recommendations and actions by Storage DRS.

Storage DRS Anti-Affinity Rules for Virtual Disks   Another useful feature of Storage DRS is the anti-affinity rule for virtual disks. This type of rule can be used to control the placement of virtual disks on datastores. There are two types of Storage DRS anti-affinity rules:

- **Inter-VM anti-affinity rule**—This rule specifies which virtual machines should never be kept on the same datastore.

- **Intra-VM anti-affinity rule**—This rule specifies which virtual disks associated with a specific virtual machine should be kept on different datastores.

Inter-VM anti-affinity rules can be used along with DRS VM anti-affinity rules to ensure that redundant applications are separated on different hosts and different datastores. Intra-VM anti-affinity rules can be used to ensure that the disk I/O for a specific VM is split across different datastores.

Storage DRS Usage Recommendations

As with any new technology, you should test how thoroughly Storage DRS will impact your infrastructure. Here are some of the advantages that Storage DRS can bring to the table:

- Storage DRS enables automatic load balancing across datastores based on I/O latency, disk space utilization, or both.

- Storage DRS anti-affinity rules can be used for more granular I/O separation or further application resiliency.

- Storage DRS enables the automatic placement of virtual machines based on I/O latency, disk space utilization, or both.

- Fully Automated Storage DRS allows Maintenance mode for a datastore. The virtual machines on the datastore will be relocated on another datastore.

Here are some general recommendations for Storage DRS:

- Fully automate Storage DRS, but measure the impact it has on your environment.

- When creating datastore clusters, keep the storage features as homogeneous as possible.

- If array hardware acceleration is used through vStorage API for Array Integration (VAAI), then do not mix datastores using this feature with those that are not.

- Replicated datastores cannot be mixed with non-replicated datastores in the same datastore cluster.

- Use Storage DRS Anti-Affinity Rules sparingly to add resiliency or separate disk I/O because they can cause troubleshooting automated Storage DRS to be more difficult.

Storage DRS and Automatic Sub-LUN Storage Tiering   At the time of this writing, Storage DRS is not aware of underlying array technologies like automatic Sub-LUN storage tiering (auto-tiering). Auto-tiering may be implemented differently by different vendors, so making Storage DRS aware of these underlying array technologies is probably not a trivial task.

The purpose of both Storage DRS and array auto-tiering technology is to dynamically and intelligently provide performance and load balancing in the most efficient manner possible. To that end, some of their features may seem redundant. Some general characteristics of auto-tiering solutions are as follows:

- Workloads can be broken apart and moved at the storage block level.

- Over time, as disk I/O patterns are discovered, "hot" blocks requiring more performance can move to higher performing storage (e.g. SSDs).

- Any change in the I/O patterns may cause different block migration recommendations to occur.

With these characteristics in mind, let's look at how fully automated Storage DRS may affect auto-tiering solutions in the following scenario:

- **Auto-tiering**—Over time, blocks of a virtual machine are determined to be "hot" and are migrated to SSDs within a storage pool.

- **Storage DRS**—An automatic migration recommendation occurs and the virtual machine is migrated via storage vMotion to a different auto-tiered datastore.

- **Auto-tiering**—The virtual machine may be viewed as an entirely new workload. As a result, the virtual machine's blocks will likely be placed on lower-performing storage depending on the auto-tiering policy of the array.

The previous scenario is what might generally happen with any Storage DRS recommendation. I/O latency recommendations combined with auto-tiering datastores may be even more complicated. Let's take a look at how I/O latency load balancing can be affected by auto-tiering: .

- **Storage DRS**—I/O latency load balancing performs random read I/O to datastores to determine latency.

- **Storage DRS**—Datastores are compared against one another to rank performance based on I/O latency.

- **Storage DRS**—Generally speaking, a datastore backed by 15 spindles will have lower latency than a datastore backed by 5 or 10 spindles. The relationship between I/O latency and spindles becomes less apparent in an auto-tiering solution.

- **Auto-tiering**—A Virtual Storage Pool may be composed of SSDs, SAS, and SATA disks.

- **Auto-tiering**—If blocks are being moved around by the auto-tiering array, the random read I/O that Storage DRS uses may be hitting SATA one time and SSDs another time. This has the potential to confuse the Storage DRS mechanism and cause it to make incorrect I/O latency migration recommendations.

Based on these characteristics, consider the following recommendations when dealing with auto-tiering and Storage DRS:

- Always consult the storage array vendor's documentation for any Storage DRS recommendations specific to that array.

- If Storage DRS is going to be used at the Fully Automatic automation level, then disable I/O latency load balancing.

We realize that disk space load balancing will still generate migration recommendations and potentially cause virtual machine blocks to land on lower-performing storage within the auto-tiering storage pool until an auto-tiering recommendation and migration can occur. However, when it comes to datastore space, we would rather see a degradation in performance than an interruption in service. When a datastore runs out of space, virtual machines will start suspending until space is freed up.

Profile-Driven Storage

If you have been working with VMware for a while, you will have seen a powerful progression in the automation capabilities of the product suite. The more automation and compliance that can be off-loaded to the software instead of the administrators, the better. Compliance to performance Service Level Agreements (SLAs) and redundancy should not be susceptible to human error. Although a competent administrator can manage this if given enough time and resources, that solution does not scale well.

Over the years, VMware has introduced features to help the administrator alleviate some of the administrative overhead that running a virtual infrastructure entails. From a host perspective, it started with DRS. DRS enabled automated load balancing and performance management for the virtual infrastructure. With vSphere 5, Storage DRS was introduced to automate load balancing and performance management from a storage perspective. What about performance or protection compliance?

This is where profile-driven storage can help. Profile-driven storage is new to vSphere 5. This feature can help to ensure that a virtual machine is only placed on storage that meets certain criteria. This criteria can be user defined, derived from the storage array itself, or both. An example of a system storage capability that is derived from the storage array itself can be seen in Figure 1.10.

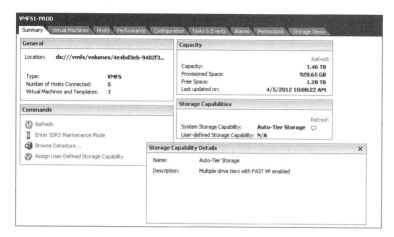

Figure 1.10 System Storage Capability

Let's take a look at an example of this feature in action.

In this scenario, a virtual machine will become a database server. The performance SLA dictates that this particular virtual machine needs to reside on RAID-10 storage that is replicated. How would you accomplish this compliance before profile-driven storage? Here is one scenario that should be familiar:

1. The storage administrator would present storage to the vSphere cluster for the vSphere administrator to utilize.

2. If the vSphere administrator asked the storage administrator for the appropriate characteristics, then he would be presented with a datastore that is RAID 10 and replicated (either to the same array or a remote array).

3. The vSphere administrator might give the datastore a descriptive name like VMFS01-RAID10-REP to denote the capabilities of the storage.

4. When deploying the virtual machine, the vSphere administrator must choose the appropriate datastore based on knowledge that he possesses about the datastore or by trusting the datastore name accurately represents the storage capabilities.

5. The vSphere administrator may put that virtual machine's details in a spreadsheet that denotes what the storage capabilities for that virtual machine should be.

6. After the virtual machine is deployed, maintaining compliance for that virtual machine can be a challenge because the compliance must be checked manually by the vSphere administrator if he has time. The vSphere administrator may consult the spreadsheet, hoping that it is up to date, to determine what storage each virtual machine should be on. Then, the vSphere administrator may look at the datastores and cross-reference the spreadsheet for compliance.

More often than not, this particular exercise may not occur at all due to the time and research required. What if the virtual machines have been migrated with storage vMotion? How many virtual machines must be checked for compliance? What if the environment consists of hundreds or thousands of virtual machines?

Now, let's look at the same scenario using profile-driven storage:

1. The storage administrator would present storage to the vSphere cluster for the vSphere administrator to utilize.

2. If the vSphere administrator asked the storage administrator for the appropriate characteristics, then he would be presented with a datastore that is RAID 10 and replicated (either to the same array or a remote array).

3. If the array supported the vStorage APIs for Array Awareness (VASA), then the array might present a "tag" (text string) for array capabilities that shows generally what the storage on the array is capable of or some of the attributes of the particular storage. VASA provided capabilities in profile-driven storage are called system capabilities. For example, the system capabilities might show as RAID10:Replicated.

4. The vSphere administrator might create a storage profile with a user-defined tag, a system capability tag, or both. For this example, let's say the user creates a Storage Profile called "Database" that uses the system capability of RAID10:Replicated.

5. When the vSphere administrator deploys the virtual machine, he may select the "Database" storage profile. After this is selected, the interface will only show those datastores (or datastore clusters if using Storage DRS) that are compliant with the "Database" storage profile. That is RAID 10 and replicated.

6. Because the storage profile is tied to the virtual machine, the infrastructure becomes self-documenting.

When compliance needs to be checked, the vSphere administrator can simply view the profile compliance status of the virtual machine. If it is out of compliance, it will be readily apparent in the vCenter interface.

Profile-driven storage helps to automate and enforce performance and protection compliance from a storage perspective. We recommend using profile-driven storage to maintain compliance in the infrastructure instead of relying on human-driven compliance checks.

Laying the Groundwork Summary

In this chapter, you reviewed the importance of laying a proper foundation for the virtual infrastructure. There is a great deal of planning that accompanies a virtual infrastructure project. You need to perform some level of capacity planning to know what hardware you will need for the project. You need to determine the requirements, constraints, and assumptions for the solution. Along those lines, some questions need to be asked:

- What type of architecture (traditional 1GbE, converged rackmount, converged blade) is most appropriate for the solution?

- Do you have the environmental requirements to deploy the solution (for example, space, power, and cooling)?

- How will you provide redundancy for the solution?

- How will you provide security for the solution?

- Are there application licensing implications that you need to consider in the solution?

- Will you take advantage of advanced vSphere features like Storage DRS? If so, does your design need to change to accommodate those features?

These questions are just examples of the types of questions you should be asking while planning a vSphere deployment. You need to make many design decisions, provide justification for those decisions, and understand the impact of those decisions on the overall design. The more you can plan in the beginning, the more solid the infrastructure foundation.

Many decisions need to be made before taking the first steps toward implementation. After this considerable planning effort, if all of the stakeholders in the project are in agreement on the design, then the implementation can begin. Chapter 2, "Implementing the Solution," will focus on implementing the design after you have planned for a solid infrastructure foundation.

Chapter 2

Implementing the Solution

Chapter 1, "Laying the Groundwork," laid the foundation for a virtualization infrastructure that will deliver not only on today's requirements but also allow for growth into the coming years.

This chapter focuses on the implementation of the solution. We go through the process of following the design blueprint and finish with checking our implementation for mistakes. In between, we talk about some of the considerations of being the implementer of the solution. The implementer of the solution might or might not also be the design engineer and we talk about both circumstances. In many cases, it is irrelevant as similar processes need to be followed either way.

We also talk about a number of real-life cases where things did not go as desired and talk about what could have—and should have—been done to avoid such issues. It is important to note that although some of this is directly relevant to a solution that has just been implemented using the processes described in Chapter 1, the information is also relevant to an infrastructure that might not have been designed with the understanding of the concepts and methodologies outlined in the previous chapter.

Following the Design Blueprint

The design blueprint refers to a set of documentation containing configurations, procedures, and processes that are being implemented. This documentation is a result of the design phase of the project with its roots in the functional requirements for the design. Although this section is not about the design, it is important to reiterate the importance of the functional requirements. Functional requirements are not something that will be handed over on a sheet of paper to you. Gathering them requires reviews with both stake-holders and technical staff.

As the implementer of a vSphere-based design, you might have been the designer as well. In this case, you will have a set of design documentation that you created and will be familiar with the functional requirements as defined. In other cases, you might be following the design blueprint that has been provided to you by another member of your organization. In either case, it is important to review the design deliverables before proceeding with the implementation.

Reviewing the Design Documentation

The design documentation should consist of the following at a minimum:

- Pre- and postimplementation performance comparison
- Site survey documentation
- Architecture documentation
- Design blueprint based on capacity planning results
- Design implementation procedures
- Design verification
- Installation and configuration procedures
- Application test procedures
- Operating procedures and guidelines
- Stakeholder review meeting notes

Some of these will end up being deliverables to stakeholders while some will only be part of a guided transition between the design and implementation persons or teams. They range in depth and breadth of being simple diagrams that may depict logical or physical viewpoints of the design to detailed information on port group configurations and settings. It is necessary to have both low- and high-level viewpoints of the design to ensure a successful implementation.

Stakeholder Review

A stakeholder review can happen several times throughout the design process. The initial importance of the stakeholder review is in gathering information that helps define the functional requirements of the design. Further reviews with stakeholders serve to verify the design is meeting these functional requirements while taking into consideration the constraints placed on the design and any associated assumptions. For example, many times we are dealing with timelines or budgets that constrain the design. This results in functional requirements that are not going to be met but need to be identified and discussed with stakeholders. These discussions with stakeholders are at a high level initially until a full technical review of the constraints and assumptions has occurred.

The result of these meetings and the process should be fully documented in the design documentation and presented as a deliverable. The main purpose of this is to clarify the design decisions made. This may be for present use or future use. Although a sign-off process should occur and everyone should understand the design decisions that were made, that does not always happen. As a result, it is necessary to have historical documentation on the justifications behind not meeting certain functional requirements. This need could occur any time from implementation to months later down the line.

It is also necessary to have a good understanding of these decisions by the implementing engineer when different from the design engineer. The following sections speak more about technical reviews, which help fill this gap. Verbal conversations, though, fail to capture the entirety of a situation and documented knowledge of the decisions is critical to accurately following an implementation plan. Ultimately, you must be able to communicate to stakeholders the changes that occurred. A failure to do so may result in a misunderstanding of the current solution being implemented and a lack of understanding of why a functional requirement was not met.

Functional Requirements

The primary end result of stakeholder reviews is the definition of the functional requirements for the project. A design seeks to meet its functional requirements while taking into consideration constraints to the design. Not all functional requirements need to be met, but the goal should be to do so.

Functional requirements are unique to an organization's project. With that said, several functional requirements are common for virtualization projects:

- Reduction of physical server real estate
- Reduction of power costs associated with many physical servers and associated costs of cooling those servers
- Reduction of total cost of ownership
- Enablement of High Availability
- Enablement of dynamically balanced workloads
- Enablement of a disaster recovery solution

Constraints

Items that limit your design are considered constraints. You should outline constraints in your design documentation and review them to make sure all constraints have been fully identified. Reviews with stakeholders are also a great time to discuss constraints as the design progresses. Proper designs identify how constraints violate other requirements of the design and the effect that such constraints will have on the design. It should be noted that existence of a constraint does not mean the constraint has to exist. Whether political or technical, an effort should be made to explore removing the constraint.

NOTE

It is important to note that during a virtualization project, items not part of the project often creep in. These are different than constraints and the functional requirements they constrain. These creeps of scope should be left for another project to ensure the focus is on meeting the functional requirements of the project as designed.

Again, documentation of constraints in the design is critical for both a historical understanding of the decisions made and as information to be utilized during the deployment. Thinking about constraints is often left to the design phase of the project and not always considered during or directly after the implementation. This is a mistake that can be avoided, though. Consider the following case.

Constraints Case Study

A solution has been designed for an environment where a major limitation has been identified in terms of available networking infrastructure to support the 12 new vSphere hosts. In conversations with the network administrator, it was revealed that there was a major constraint in terms of available gigabit network ports. Unfortunately, despite discussing the benefits that a server with six NICs would have, the additional switching that would need to be purchased to support the infrastructure was deemed unnecessary at this time for a virtualization initiative. With all the systems that will be decommissioned when they are converted from physical to virtual, there would be ports freed on the switching, but, unfortunately, these have all been identified as Fast Ethernet (10/100 Mb) ports. The servers are ordered with the six NICs as desired as a result of the increased benefits of redundancy that can be accomplished. Only four of the six NICs, however, will be hooked into the gigabit switching at the datacenter.

As a result of the networking constraints, the design lays out the management network spread across two Fast Ethernet switches. The remaining four ports are set up for virtual machine networking, vMotion, and IP storage networking. With six NICs hooked into a gigabit infrastructure, we normally would take management traffic and place it down the same set of networking as vMotion traffic because those two traffic types are the two that will play together nicely the best. With the constraint of Fast Ethernet networking, this is not possible. With the need to use IP-based storage to support NFS, the design will place IP-based storage on a single, dedicated NIC as will vMotion. For both of these, the other's active NIC will be used as its standby. The remaining two NICs for each server will be dedicated for virtual machine networking traffic. This might not be an ideal design, but it meets the functional requirements of the customer considering the constraints we have in networking.

As with any organization, things change and multiple projects tend to occur at the same time. Often, different teams or even individuals on the same team might fail to keep the other one in the loop. Perhaps both individuals are just so busy that they don't really have the time to discuss what is currently going on. In this case, the latter occurred.

It turned out another long-standing project had an impact on the network infrastructure that would be in place before the implementation was completed. The other project had to do with a turnkey vendor–provided solution that was now being upgraded. It consisted of more than ten physical servers, which, of course, in turn required a lot of network ports. Fast Ethernet ports were in abundance, but with the new version of the solution, gigabit networking for the switching was now required. They balked at the solution and chose to hold off on the upgrade until the vendor came down in pricing and, lo and behold, additional gigabit switching was added to their infrastructure.

Even though the individual working on the turnkey solution project was involved in the original design discussions and knew the vSphere design could really use the faster networking for all of its ports, months had passed and this constraint that was put into place had long been forgotten.

Unfortunately, by the time this came to light, production workloads were already placed on the infrastructure so individual vSphere hosts did have some down time. Thanks to the technologies within vSphere, the use of Maintenance mode and vMotion ensured that none of the virtual workloads had any down time. With careful planning, the design was changed and documented to provide a much more reliable and quicker networking access for each of the hosts all around.

This is a case where some due diligence leads to a big win. Thanks to following a process where we always verify our work throughout the process, even our constraints, we were able to resolve a less-desirable part of the design that no longer had to be the way it was.

Technology changes fast and, as a result, so do many things about an infrastructure. This case could have easily gone the other way and someone working on the other project could have taken up all those gigabit networking ports before the vSphere implementation took place. Always be cognizant that many things are going on in an organization's technology infrastructure at any given time. What you are working on will be affected by the work of others. Your actions will also have the same effect on others' work.

Constraints will be different for every organization and every project, but there are several common constraints for virtualization projects:

- Vendor preference

- Budget

- Organizational best practices and policies

- Government regulations

- Existing network infrastructure (that is, the lack of gigabit or 10-gigabit networking or limited networking capacity)

- Existing storage infrastructure (that is, the presence of only a certain type of storage with limited capabilities, limited performance, or limited space available)

- Existing host hardware

Technical Review

A technical review can occur several times throughout the design process. Technical reviews should be focused on meeting the functional requirements of the business while considering the constraints. Whether considered formal or not, you will find that you perform technical reviews following any stakeholder review. These may take form via simple verbal communication or may be a formal meeting. Regardless, any time a discussion about functional requirements and constraints occurs, a later discussion will take place to consider technical ramifications and how to proceed with the design and implementation. The process will occur several times, with updates being done to the design after each technical review iteration.

Technical reviews are a good time to review all assumptions before proceeding with an implementation. The goal should be to resolve as many of the assumptions as possible to eliminate the risk that assumptions themselves pose. Regardless of the formality of the meetings, they should be documented and distributed to all stakeholders. This documentation should be targeted. For example, the appropriate documentation will be much different for end users than for technical individuals involved with the project or senior management.

Assumptions

Assumptions in a vSphere design are no different than assumptions in any other part of our life. To make headway with a design, it is often necessary to make certain assumptions. You may assume that your installation media for Windows Server 2008 will be available on the network for installation, or you may assume that adequate network bandwidth will exist for a disaster recovery solution using storage-based replication. Regardless, it is important to have a list of assumptions for the design.

Failing to have the list of assumptions is one problem. Another is a failure to review these assumptions immediately before the implementation of the solution. In many instances, assumptions are items that may be put back on stakeholders, customers, or others for follow-up or completion. Rudimentary items like not having Windows installation media, licensing information, or network cables make it impossible to get past the initial steps of an implementation plan. These failures typically cause hours of lost time. Other items can cost you days or even weeks. For example, consider the following scenario.

Assumptions Case Study

A design is needed to virtualize 150 existing physical servers. These servers are located throughout various branch offices and the business wants to centralize them at its main datacenter, which currently hosts four other existing physical servers. The business is asking for virtualization as a means to reduce its server footprint and save on hardware and power costs. Additionally, the business is requiring the capability to tolerate hardware failures and limited growth within its environment.

Without going into the specifics based on capacity planning results and the required average and peak workloads, you find you are able to virtualize nearly all the physical systems onto 11 rackmount servers. This takes into account both the required average and peak workloads as well as two additional hosts that are provided for growth and redundancy. In the end, it is also determined that two of the four existing physical servers at the main datacenter must remain physical due to internal business policies and vendor supportability.

It is late into the first day of the implementation and you are just finishing up the cabling of the eleventh server. After all that cabling, you think to yourself, "boy, it would have been nice if they bought blades." You begin powering on the servers one by one and as you begin to hear the loud blast of fans from the sixth server, you then hear the opposite all around you. The UPS tripped due to a load it couldn't handle. The sound of silence in a datacenter is something you don't often hear, but it is something you will have to hear about if you are involved.

Maybe as the implementer it wasn't your fault. You look at the design documentation after the dust settles and see the assumption listed, "Customer has existing UPS that can handle the load of the existing servers. Customer will verify with vendor peak load and acquire additional UPS if needed."

Although it might be true the customer failed to verify the UPS, the implementer has the responsibility to verify these items before implementation. This is the case even if an assumption wasn't listed in the design documentation. In this case, a good place to start would have been to check the model of the UPS. Further verification could have been accomplished by physically checking the UPS's load. Issues with implementing the vSphere solution didn't just hinder the new infrastructure in this case, but brought down the existing physical infrastructure as well.

Assumptions have to be made; you cannot possibly check everything. For some things, however, assumptions should never be made. This is especially true as you consider increasing consolidation ratios in your vSphere deployments. Consider reviewing all assumptions during an assurance review so that all assumptions are understood and signed off on. As the design or implementation engineer, you can trust that the assumption holds true, but you must also verify that it holds true.

Design Deviations

It has been established that at times it might be necessary to deviate from the original intention of the design. Many times, this is the result of a change in functional requirements. Other times, assumptions that were made about the existing environment might have ended up being invalid. Either way, the net result is the same. Something has changed within the environment and it must be properly documented. Furthermore, this change will have an effect on the rest of the implementation and must be properly considered.

When Functional Requirements Change

Functional requirements may continually change during the design phase of a vSphere deployment. These changes can be easily dealt with by properly adjusting and reevaluating the design with any new constraints that the new functional requirements may pose. If the functional requirements begin to change during an implementation, it might be time to formally reengage stakeholders to validate whether the new functional requirements need to be integrated now or postponed until later. There are certainly cases for both depending on the functional requirements that have changed.

Continuing the Implementation Case Study

You are rolling along with your implementation and have about half of the physical servers already converted to virtual machines. In just several months, you'll be finished with the project.

Significant time has already been spent up until this point in creating a design that considers a multitude of factors. Functional requirements have been balanced with constraints to come up with a polished design and implementation plan. Any deviations from this can pose serious risk to the successful implementation of the design. You now are approached about virtualizing even more of the infrastructure than originally intended.

When the solution was designed, it took into account just a portion of the business. With the business operating under several divisions, it has been hard to come to a consensus on a road map for the datacenter and, specifically, virtualization technologies. One division decided it would look in to building its own infrastructure and building a proof of concept for Hyper-V. Therefore, a plan was put in place to move forward based on the assumption that certain servers would be virtualized.

A capacity planner was performed and the information generated was collected and analyzed. This resulted in a design that fully met the functional requirements of the business. A problem arises, though. The proof of concept the other division started didn't match its needs. Knowing the vSphere infrastructure would be set up and ready for more virtual machines also makes the other division think again about deploying its own separate physical servers in the future. Furthermore, with recent initiatives to reduce costs, initiatives have come down to begin consolidating systems to reduce the amount of excess server capacity that is wasted as a result of administrators operating in silos.

The business now wants to virtualize all of the systems together. There is a problem, though, in terms of capacity. The original design was to virtualize 100 servers plus room for growth over the next three years. The new requirements add another 100 servers to the infrastructure, making it impossible to meet the new infrastructure being deployed as designed.

Fortunately, your boss understands that you'll need much more in your infrastructure than you currently have in terms of hosts, CPU, memory, and storage. He says there is room in the budget and you should be able to double the hosts with matching CPU and memory configurations and expand the storage array to meet the capacity of the systems being newly introduced.

After talking with your boss, you give the go-ahead to move along with the implementation despite the new requirements. You are not worried, though, because you now will have double the resources available.

Thanks to the help of IT admins in some of the other divisions, you quickly move through implementing and virtualizing the existing physical server workloads. As you get closer to the end of the project, you begin to receive many complaints about the performance. You hear from people that things were fine several months ago but have progressively gotten worse and worse.

A few small details are uncovered. When the first 100 systems were configured, it was discovered that memory was drastically overprovisioned as was the number of processors. Adjustments were made and then carried over to the second 100 systems that rightsized the virtual machines to match what their expected peak usage would be. It turns out the second 100 systems needed more than this. Several more physical vSphere hosts would be necessary to account for this mistake.

Memory and CPU contention is reduced, but some poor performance is still noticed. The culprit now turns out to be the storage. It turns out the second batch of systems not only used more memory and CPU, but several systems were heavily disk intensive and the infrastructure was now starved for available IOPS.

This is just one example of many we have seen where changing requirements during an implementation can cause unexpected results. In all fairness, a lot of these situations end up being the result of political issues. People who don't understand the technology are sometimes the same people in charge of making technology decisions or responsible for the budgets for technology. In reality, what started as a change in requirements should have resulted in a redesign. A Capacity Planner for the second 100 servers would have been an ideal start.

With that horror story, let's consider the case for halting the implementation.

Halting the Implementation Case Study

You have acknowledged the risk that changing the design may pose at this point, but have realized there are some things you desperately need this implementation to do. You don't have weeks or months to wait and need to begin thinking about this now.

Some individuals in this story might have sworn that the need to do this was right now. We live in a world where technology enables us to move quickly. As a result, expectations can often follow that assume such agility. Although there is often a false idea of urgency around things, there are certainly cases where things might be more immediate. Let's consider the case for halting the implementation.

You are rolling along in your implementation and are just a few weeks away from migrating your physical infrastructure over. During the design, you decided not to incorporate your Microsoft Cluster Service systems. This was a conscious choice after considering the constraints this would place on your design. In particular, the lack of support for vMotion was of most concern because this would make operating and maintaining the infrastructure more complicated.

These are the only physical systems that are to remain after the project is completed. Over a two-week period, you have noticed two drive failures, one in each of the clusters. You find the systems are out of warranty but spare drives are easily ordered and affordable.

A week later, two more fail, both of which are on the same system. However, it isn't a problem because this is a Microsoft Cluster, so everything failed over. You spend a few hours troubleshooting and are able to recover from the failure pretty easily. You certainly have a problem on your hands, though, because the hardware is out of warranty and clearly older than was originally realized. There is no room in the budget to replace the hardware anytime soon and you must react quickly.

You decide it is necessary to stop where you are and not move any of the other physical servers over so that you have enough available capacity for the Microsoft Clusters. Fortunately, several of the servers to be completed are still newer hardware that was purchased only six months prior. These systems are also not business critical and don't necessarily need to remain highly available. You check capacity and see that you have plenty available for the Microsoft Clusters. You carry over these redesign efforts to your storage where you make room for the new LUNs that will need to be created using Raw Device Mapping (RDM).

You migrate the clusters over and everything is up and running. Although you are not exceeding your capacity, you have only a little room for growth. It was probably a good thing you held off from moving any of the other workloads over and they will have to wait until the next budget cycle when you can purchase the necessary hardware.

Although everyone would agree it would have been a much worse idea to take the risk of virtualizing the workloads and exceeding capacity, there are some more details.

After you were committed to the project, a few things were uncovered that enabled you to not only virtualize the rest of the physical workloads, but also to do so without the need to purchase any additional servers. When looking at the requirements of the Microsoft Clustered Application, you found that the recovery time objective (RTO) needed hours and not minutes or seconds as MSCS is appropriate for. VMware's High Availability would easily solve this requirement. Further fault tolerance would be considered in the future if a smaller RTO was desired.

This discovery led to the first key reduction in infrastructure requirement. You were now able to reduce the virtual server imprint from these applications from four down to two. This led to some more available resources, a reduction in your Windows licensing, and the lift of some of the restrictions MSCS clusters placed on the environment. This was immediately a big win.

Although this freed up some resources, it was clear this was not going to be enough to vir-tualize all the remaining workloads. A funny thing happened when you looked at the con-figurations of some of the physical servers in play. Several of them were identical in model and configuration minus some memory to the deployed vSphere hosts. Ordering up some additional memory easily resolved that issue.

With the ordering of a few additional vSphere licenses, the infrastructure was now ready and you began assisting in moving the remaining workloads off and redeploying those matching servers into the vSphere cluster.

When Assumptions Prove Incorrect

We discussed earlier in this chapter the importance of validating certain assumptions. Those assumptions that could have a large impact on an infrastructure or pose significant delays to an implementation should always be verified. We also acknowledged that it is impossible to validate every assumption. For example, it can be very difficult to verify Windows installation media is easily available, or you might not have access to check whether adequate network ports exist to install a vSphere host as originally designed.

When you have acknowledged that an assumption you made was not correct, you then must take proper action going forward to reduce any further effect on the implemen-tation. This starts by documenting the change. Unlike a change in functional requirements that can occur, an incorrect assumption might be smaller in scale and might need to be corrected on the fly. For example, you might have assumed you have adequate network infrastructure to support the two new vSphere servers based on information provided to you.

In the previous case study, when gigabit networking became available during the project, you ended up in a positive situation. In this situation, you are now onsite and ready to deploy the solution, but you now have a change in the technological infrastructure that will be supporting the solution and you must properly document the situation and move forward as appropriate.

In an ideal world, you should have done a site survey and confirmed specific switches, blades, and ports the vSphere hosts would be plugged in to. Due to certain circumstances, this might not always be possible and situations like this will occur as a result.

It is highly recommended to complete a site survey beforehand. When possible, multiple site surveys are ideal. Two different problems tend to spawn from doing site surveys too early or too late. From our experience, not doing a site survey well in advance fails to expose critical assumptions that cause a failure in the implementation. Nothing is worse than being expected to implement on a given day and having to hold off because the required pieces are not in place. On the other hand, leaving too much time in between can pose issues as well. For example, at times network connectivity can be scarce in certain locations and unused ports have a way of finding themselves used over time, even when reserved for other usage.

Automating Implementation Tasks

Automation allows you to accomplish implementations faster and more accurately. It might not eliminate, but will greatly reduce the amount of repetitive tasks that are part of a vSphere deployment. This might be reason enough to automate certain portions of your implementation. The greatest benefit, however, is in the standardization that automation can provide.

Several methods can accomplish this. The following sections discuss a few technologies that enable such automation. Each of these methods is briefly discussed and the following sections provide some useful community resources that take advantage of automation. The sections also talk about how these technologies can even be used with each other to deliver a robust and powerful solution for automating vSphere deployments.

PowerCLI

PowerCLI is a Windows PowerShell snap-in that provides a command-line method to automate many aspects of a vSphere deployment. It is easy to learn the basics and execute your first PowerCLI script. Beyond that, it is also a useful tool for querying and generating reports about an existing vSphere infrastructure. Although Microsoft really hit the nail on the head with the PowerShell language, the real power of the technology for vSphere environments is in the many scripts and learning resources that have been shared among the VMware community.

Throughout this book, several PowerShell scripts are provided that will aid in implementing, managing, and operating your environment. Learning PowerShell is beyond the scope of this book, but if you are looking to become familiar with PowerCLI, you can refer to Appendix A at the back of this book, which provides a list of excellent resources on this topic.

Host Profiles

Host Profiles are a feature of vCenter that allows profiles to be created and applied to vSphere hosts. Host Profiles ease configuration management of your vSphere hosts and provide the ability to monitor and check against configuration drift. This feature is part of the Enterprise Plus Edition only.

During an implementation, Host Profiles are great for automating the application of configuration to your hosts. After that, we rarely see them used for continuous verification and alerting of noncompliance. This isn't due to a lack of capability but rather a lack of knowledge of the product. Many people don't realize that a task can be scheduled to check compliance of a profile individual times or on a recurring basis. Additionally, alerts can be generated to confirm the host is compliant, noncompliant, or that the compliance check has occurred.

By default, profiles are checked once a day via a scheduled task that is created for each profile when it is created. Like alerts , there isn't any email notification by default and this must be configured. You may configure email notification to confirm the task itself has completed by editing the scheduled task. You probably already get enough email every day though and want to know specifically when things are problematic. You can get this level of granularity through the use of alarms that are configured for email notification.

You may configure notification for Host Profile application, compliance, and noncompliance at the vCenter, datacenter, cluster, or host level. First, select the appropriate level of hierarchy you want to configure. Next, create a new alarm and go to

> Alarm Settings, Alarm Type: Hosts, Monitor for Specific Events, Triggers: Host Profile Applied, Host Compliant with Profile, Host Noncompliant with Profile

You may configure notification to ensure cluster compliance is being checked as well. This can be done at the vCenter, datacenter, or cluster level. First, select the appropriate level of hierarchy you want to configure. Next, create a new alarm and go to

> Alarm Settings, Alarm Type: Clusters, Monitor for Specific Events, Triggers: Check Cluster for Compliance

---

DEPLOYMENT TIP

When you first install vSphere, you have a 60-day grace period before applying your license. If you aren't using the Enterprise Plus Edition, this is a great time to try some of the features, such as Auto Deploy and the distributed virtual switch. In the case of Host Profiles, this is a great time to not only try the feature, but also to save some time during the implementation. When you are finished configuring the first host, simply create a Host Profile and then attach it to the rest of your cluster. After it has applied, it will be configured just like the other hosts.

Auto Deploy Server

vSphere 5 has added the capability to automatically provision hosts through the use of an Auto Deploy Server. Auto Deploy is a new feature in vSphere 5 that auto provisions hosts in the infrastructure. The Auto Deploy Server in many ways turns the vSphere host's hardware into a commodity. It does so by deploying a stateless image that runs from memory. You may choose to run Update Manager to do patches that don't require reboot only. Remember that these hosts are stateless and will load the unmodified boot image at load time, effectively wiping out any changes that were made that aren't part of a Host Profile. Instead, you would simply update the host image using Image Builder.

The Auto Deploy Server requires Enterprise Plus licensing; however, there is an offset in costs that will result from eliminating local storage from the servers.

Auto Deploy also requires some additional infrastructure components that might or might not already exist. As depicted in Figure 2.1, these include DHCP, PXE, TFTP, and PowerCLI. The process for setting up Auto Deploy is documented by VMware in the *vSphere 5 Evaluation Guide, Volume Four*, the link for which is provided in Appendix A. A common place of error is during the DHCP scope configuration.

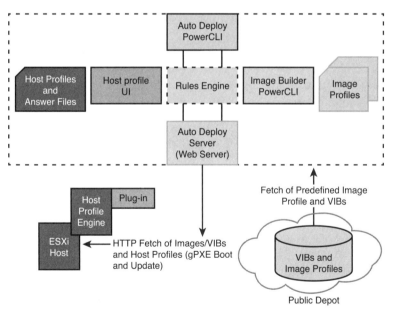

Figure 2.1   Auto Deploy Components

For a Windows DHCP scope, you must configure both options 66 and 67, as noted in Figure 2.2. Option 66 will specify the TFTP server while option 67 will be the bootfile name, which should be undionly.kpxe.vmw-hardwired.

Option Name	Vendor	Value	Class
003 Router	Standard	192.168.1.1	None
006 DNS Servers	Standard	192.168.1.80, 192.168.1.81	None
015 DNS Domain Name	Standard	vmware.com	None
066 Boot Server Host Name	Standard	192.168.1.31	None
067 Bootfile Name	Standard	undionly.kpxe.vmw-hardwired	None

Figure 2.2   Configuring Windows DHCP Scope for Auto Deploy

For a Cisco DHCP scope, there can be some difficulty in making the configurations, especially if you are less familiar with Cisco networking. Not to worry as there are only two lines you need to configure for the scope. *Next-server* refers to the TFTP server you have configured, while *bootfile* refers to the bootfile name, which should be undionly.kpxe.vmw-hardwired.

```
Router(config)# ip dhcp pool My-Pool
Router(dhcp-config)# next-server 192.168.1.44
Router(dhcp-config)# bootfile undionly.kpxe.vmw-hardwired
```

Auto Deploy was originally released by VMware Labs as a fling before being incorporated into the most recent release of vCenter. In that release, Auto Deploy was an appliance that incorporated a TFTP server. With the release of Auto Deploy for vCenter 5, the TFTP server is not included and you must provide your own.

Solarwinds has a great TFTP server that will fit your needs with one caveat. By default, like many free TFTP solutions, it will not start automatically with Windows. However, this is not a problem because some of these applications, including Solarwinds, enable you to set the service to start automatically as a Windows service.

Auto Deploy has a good use case when it comes to rectifying hardware-based host failures in a vSphere cluster. This includes environments where host failover capacity is not purchased or the environments that want extra hardware ready and available in the case of several hardware failures.

Auto Deploy delivers pieces based on deployment rules that are defined by patterns. Simply defining patterns based on the host hardware type of some older, but still fully supported, hardware would allow another host to be fully set up with patches like the rest of your hosts. Additionally, once online, Host Profiles will finish the setup and standardize the host as you have chosen.

Of course, you also need to make sure the host has the same processor type/level as the existing cluster or enable the Enhanced vMotion capability. Sure, this capability to bring another host online exists without the use of Auto Deploy, but it is important to remember that not all infrastructures being built will have someone available to go through all the steps in the process to bring a host online and integrate it into the vSphere infrastructure. Even those that do might not have had any hands-on time with vSphere in some time. Being set up for Auto Deploy in this case means you've taken the time beforehand to ensure everything will be ready to go when it is needed most. Times of crisis are times when a lot is learned, but that doesn't mean they always have to be.

vCenter Orchestrator

vCenter Orchestrator is perhaps one of the least understood features of vCenter. We also have found it to be one of the least used features as a result. vCenter Orchestrator provides workflows that aid in automating actions. One of the core benefits of the product is it provides a library of workflows to choose from so that you are not reinventing the wheel for every automation need you might have. Products such as vCloud Director, for example, are heavily reliant on the workflows put in place for setting up a vCloud Director infrastructure. Additionally, custom workflows can be created from existing or new additions to the library. Figure 2.3 shows these components and note that it also shows vCenter Orchestrator's reliance on its own dedicated database server.

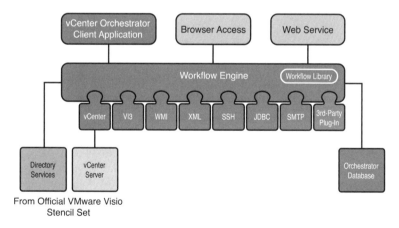

Figure 2.3 vCenter Orchestrator Components

One thing that comes as a shock to many is that vCenter Orchestrator is installed by default with vCenter and after a brief configuration is ready for your workflows. It is, however, only available with vCenter Standard Edition or above.

Detailed information on the use of vCenter Orchestrator is outside the scope of this book. Cody Bunch, however, has published a complete work on its use in his book *Automating vSphere with VMware vCenter Orchestrator*, published by VMware Press.

Verifying Implementation

The hardware has been deployed, vSphere has been installed, and you are ready to start eliminating all of those physical servers. Before going any further and placing production workloads in the infrastructure, the implementation should be verified. When talking about verifying the implementation, note that there are actually two different types of verification.

First, you need to verify the implementation for functionality. This means testing for a desired outcome. Here, you confirm items are functional under a number of scenarios outlined in your verification plan. Second, you need to verify configurations of your implementation. Again, you analyze the implementation, but this time you look to ensure your configurations match the intended design.

There are a number of scenarios in which a vSphere environment may function correctly in the current state yet not match the intended configurations. Note that when you test functionality, you are only testing against the present state. Configurations outlined in the design, however, may take into account anticipated changes to the infrastructure. Assessing both functionality and configuration helps mitigate these issues.

Testing Functionality

As previously mentioned, functionality testing will be performed to ensure features of the design function as intended. When discussing functionality, it means you are focusing on whether an item works. Furthermore, the feature needs to function at certain levels and meet set expectations of performance. A detailed list of the functionality to be tested should be included with the design documentation. Furthermore, an outlined plan of how to test each function should be produced when possible. This test plan should be updated with new releases of vSphere as subfeatures of items—like High Availability and Distributed Resource Scheduler—tend to change, and other new ones are introduced, such as Storage DRS with the release of vSphere 5.0. Whereas DRS balances virtual machines across hosts based on CPU and memory utilization of the hosts, Storage DRS balances virtual machines based not only on space usage, but also on I/O latency. Now let's talk about some of the specific functionality that should be tested during a typical vSphere implementation.

High Availability

VMware's High Availability feature, or HA, will restart virtual machines on another host in the event of a failure to a vSphere host. Additionally, a subfeature of HA known as *VM monitoring* or *VM HA* will restart a specific virtual machine if an operating system crashes. This section goes through High Availability at a high level; however, I highly recommend you check out Duncan Epping's *HA Deepdive* (see Appendix A) for a deeper understanding of configuration options.

For HA, then, you have two main features you need to verify, the ability to restart all VMs on a host and the ability to restart a specific VM that has failed.

Host Failure

To determine your functionality testing plan for HA Host failures, you need to make sure you understand the intended result of your configurations. HA is configured with a host isolation response that dictates the expected action for virtual machines if an HA failure has been detected. The isolation response will be one of the following. Note the description beside each of the available options.

- **Shut Down**—Safe shutdown of the guest after 5 minutes. This was the default in vSphere 4.1.

- **Power Off**—Hard shutdown of the guest immediately.

- **Leave Powered On**—Virtual machines remain powered on. This is the default in vSphere 5.

Now that you know the possible isolation responses, which one do you configure? In general, our recommendation is to use Leave Powered On for most scenarios. This option keeps virtual machines running if the host still has access to the storage. This is the best option for both IP-based and Fibre Channel–based storage where a host isolation wouldn't also cause an isolation from the storage. Furthermore, if the storage also becomes isolated, this option leads to a power off.

If it is possible hosts will still have access to storage during isolation and a restart is required, then choosing the Shut Down option is recommended. This provides a safe shutdown of the operating system and eliminates chances of corruption occurring to operating systems that are not cleanly dismounted.

If it is likely hosts will not have access to storage during an isolation event, then Shutdown is not going to be an option because the virtual machine cannot be accessed. This might be the case when using IP-based storage and when a network isolation would result in that connectivity being severed. When the requirement is to quickly restart virtual machines when an isolation event occurs, then the Power Off option is recommended.

Knowing the anticipated isolation response is only part of what you need to understand. You also need to know which virtual machines you are expecting to power back on and in what order. This is especially important in environments that are close to or 100% virtualized as application dependencies such as Active Directory, DNS, and SQL will prevent other machines from properly starting their own services that are dependent upon them.

Again, place close attention to noticing which virtual machines are expected to be powered back on. The design will dictate this because it might be expected that only a given set of virtual machines will be powered back on as a trade-off for reduced failover capacity. A failure to properly lay out the virtual machines that will power back on along with their order could lead to critical virtual machines being restarted later or not at all due to a violation of HA admission control settings. Consider designing a power down and restart plan as part of operational procedures. This process should include not only the order of restart of virtual machines but also application dependencies. As changes occur with applications and services over time, also consider HA settings and the effect of a host failure on applications.

Several methods exist to simulate a host failure for testing purposes:

- Remove all networking.

- Remove all power.

- For blade servers, remove the blade.

- Force a kernel panic, the Purple Screen of Death (PSOD).

Another method that also accomplishes the simulation of a host failure for purposes of testing is forcing a kernel panic, which creates a dump file. To force a kernel panic:

1. Connect to the vSphere host via SSH or the ESXi console.

2. Type **vsish**.

3. Type **set /reliability/crashMe/Panic**.

A VM that has blue screened or is otherwise unresponsive can be restarted using VM HA. To test the functionality of a virtual machine, restarting will be necessary to have a way to force a failure. This can be accomplished through a number of utilities that trigger a blue screen. You can also initiate the failure of a specific virtual machine from a vSphere host by doing the following:

1. Connect to a host using SSH.

2. As shown in Figure 2.4, determine the World ID of the virtual machine(s) to be crashed by entering the command **esxcli vm process list** and locating the value for World ID.

```
  192.168.1.41 - PuTTY
~ # esxcli vm process list
vnx01
   World ID: 3673
   Process ID: 0
   VMX Cartel ID: 3671
   UUID: 42 1f 48 49 01 1c 94 cc-bd 32 e5 42 ce 9a ca de
   Display Name: vnx01
   Config File: /vmfs/volumes/4cfd73e5-ced778aa-271b-b8ac6f957c71/vnx01/vnx01.vm
~ #
```

Figure 2.4 Forcing a Virtual Machine Failure

3. Enter the command **/sbin/vmdumper** *wid* **nmi** where *wid* represents the World ID
    of the virtual machine to which you would like to send the NMI.

Distributed Resource Scheduler

VMware's Distributed Resource Scheduler (DRS) dynamically balances your resources
among vSphere hosts. It accomplishes this via the use of resource pools and allows several
levels of automation to take action based on recommendations provided. Recommendations that are provided range from priority 1 to 5, with 1 being the most conservative
and 5 being the most aggressive. The automation levels available are manual, partially
automated, and fully automated. As discussed earlier in Chapter 1, the recommended
setting is fully automated unless a constraint exists that deems otherwise.

Several subfeatures of DRS exist. These include affinity and anti-affinity rules, DRS
groups, Distributed Power Management (DPM), and automation levels for individual
VMs.

DRS groups allow the creation of two different kinds of groups, host groups and virtual
machine groups. When testing the functionality of DRS, the main objective is to ensure
DRS is functioning by moving virtual machines during times of contention. This is accomplished when vMotion operations are initiated.

To accomplish this, you need to simulate a high load on a host, which can be easily accomplished by spiking the utilization of CPU on individual virtual machines. You could also
seek to utilize memory on virtual machines; however, it will typically take many more
virtual machines to cause contention with memory than it will to cause contention with the
processor. Many tools exist to accomplish these actions, and two that we recommend are
as follows:

- **CPUbusy**—There are many variations of this script. The software will spike the
  CPU on a virtual machine while running and cause near 100% utilization.

- **Heavyload**—This software performs CPU, memory, and disk load to aid in testing
  performance.

One thing that might come to light here as well is issues with virtual machines or hosts that are not configured correctly to enable vMotion. Running a separate test ahead of time to check for vMotion compatibility is a good idea and you learn more about this later in the chapter.

Networking

When testing networking functionality, you must verify functionality across a number of areas. With the use of IP-based storage, this means you need to verify storage functionality in addition to the networking components they consist of.

For a vSwitch, two types of network port groups can be created. A virtual machine port group can contain only virtual machines, and only virtual machines can be in a virtual machine port group. A VMkernel port group, on the other hand, can be used for one or several types of traffic:

- Management
- Virtual machine
- vMotion
- FT
- Storage networking (either iSCSI or NFS)

Each of these different types of networks requires unique plans for testing functionality because they differ in functionality themselves. Let's start our functionality verification at the management level.

Verifying Management Networking Functionality

Of all the traffic types that can be configured for a VMkernel port, management traffic is the only one that is required to be configured for at least one of the VMkernel ports on a host. A single VMkernel port might not be ideal and you might choose to configure a second VMkernel port that is configured with a different set of outbound NICs backed by separate network infrastructure from the first VMkernel port. You might also decide like many that a second VMkernel port entails a more complex configuration and implementation and that the risk of a VMkernel port failing is fairly low. In this case, a single VMkernel port for management backed by a set of multiple NICs that are part of a separate network infrastructure might meet your requirements.Regardless of how your management network is configured, you need to make sure it is functional at all times. The best way to do this is to verify redundancy, the process of which is described in the following steps:

1. Disconnect one of the two management networks. If your implementation consists of two VMkernel ports, remove the network connectivity to one of those ports. If your implementation consists of a single VMkernel port backed by multiple physical network adapters, remove network connectivity to one of those adapters.

2. Verify management connectivity still exists to the host. This can be done by pinging the host or connecting with the vSphere client.

3. Reconnect the management network that was disconnected.

4. Disconnect the other management network.

5. Verify management connectivity to the host still exists.

6. Reconnect the management network that was disconnected.

If this test fails, it is likely you have not configured the management port group correctly or one of the management networks is not configured properly end to end.

You need to ensure that you have configured the vmnics for the management port group in a manner that allows for proper failover. If you mistakenly configured a vmnic as an unused adapter, then this test will always fail. We recommend an active/active setup for the management port group. Earlier we discussed a recommendation of two NICs dedicated to management traffic; however, we understand this might not always be the case. You might have fewer physical NICs to use and as a result, you might then have shared NICs for management with vMotion traffic. In this case, you need to check and ensure the port group is configured in an active/standby fashion, with the active NIC for management being the standby NIC for vMotion and vice versa.

Verifying Virtual Machine Networking Functionality

Creating a virtual infrastructure is without purpose if virtual machines cannot run uninhibited, so checking the functionality of the virtual machine networking is critical to any project. When you look at virtual machine networking, you are going to be concerned with not only whether it works, but also whether it is performing to your expectations. Additionally, you need to verify redundancy and the ability to failback after a failover if required. Security is also important, and you must ensure you are isolating virtual machines as required by the requirement of the design.

Verifying Virtual Machine Networking Isolation

If any of the virtual machines are to be isolated from other virtual machines, it is necessary to verify these machines cannot talk to each other. For some environments, this might be few or no virtual machines that are isolated from others. In other environments, there might be many machines isolated from each other using Private Virtual Local Area

Networks (PVLAN) or vShield Zones. Verify network connectivity does not exist for any or all services that are supposed to be blocked. This can be done by attempting to communicate to other hosts or networks that are designed to be isolated.

Furthermore, any machines that need to talk to each other should have their communication with each other verified. This will be a majority of your virtual machines.

Verifying Virtual Machine Networking Redundancy and Failback

Verifying virtual machine networking redundancy is similar to the verification of management networking redundancy you ran through earlier. You should do the following for each virtual machine network that exists:

1. Define several virtual machines to test with. Issue a continuous ping to each system and verify connectivity currently exists.

2. Disconnect one of virtual machine network vmnics.

3. Verify connectivity still exists to the virtual machines.

4. Reconnect the vmnic that was disconnected.

5. Disconnect another vmnic.

6. Verify connectivity still exists to the virtual machines.

7. Reconnect the vmnic that was disconnected.

8. Repeat for each vmnic that backs the virtual machine network port group.

If this test fails, it is likely you have not configured the virtual machine port group correctly or one of the network links is not configured properly end to end. Additionally, you might not have properly defined the active and/or standby vmnics properly.

Verifying Virtual Machine Networking Performance

You will test virtual machine networking performance from the perspective of the guest operating system. To do this, you use a tool such as iPerf, which allows performing tests end to end from multiple servers or workstations.

Of course for this testing, the expected results depend on what type of network connectivity exists end to end. Even with 10-gigabit networking, if the source and destination have to be routed through a 1-gigabit router, you cannot expect anything higher than the smallest link in terms of throughput. On the flip side, two virtual machines that exist on the same host will have the greatest possible throughput with each other.

From a single virtual machine, check the throughput as follows:

- With another virtual machine on the same host
- With another virtual machine on a different host
- With another machine on a different subnet

From multiple virtual machines, check the throughput as follows:

- With other virtual machines on the same host
- With other virtual machines on different hosts
- With other virtual machines on different subnets

Checking individual virtual machine networking can be tedious and there is another way to ensure that networking is not being saturated from the vmnic level. From each host, you can use esxtop and look at the networking performance for each vmnic.

From the vSphere host, either logged in remotely or at the console, you can load esxtop by entering **esxtop** at the Command Line Interface (CLI). Additionally, you can use resxtop when using the remote CLI or the vSphere Management Appliance (vMA). Once loaded, you can enter the network view by typing **n**. You might notice a high number of packets of data being transmitted; however, the biggest indicator of network saturation tends to be dropped packets. Anything over zero is an indicator of issues for either dropped packets transmitted (%DRPTX) or dropped packets received (%DRPRX).

A full lesson on esxtop is beyond the scope of this book; however, refer to Appendix A for a great esxtop learning resource.

Verifying vMotion Networking Functionality

vMotion networking differs from the other types of networking required in that it has high requirements for throughput while having occasional or rare use in some environments. As a result, it is best to dedicate network adapters strictly for vMotion to not only give it the throughput it needs, but also to ensure it does not contend with other critical virtual machine or IP storage traffic.

Verifying vMotion Works

Several things can cause a vMotion attempt to fail even if the networking is correctly configured. You might have a CD-ROM drive attached to an ISO file that the destination does not have or a network configured or named differently on the destination host. It can be tedious to check these all out ahead of time manually, but you can use PowerShell and some of the many great resources already out there to ensure all of your virtual machines are capable of moving to any host.

Please refer to Appendix A for a scripted resource to test vMotion.

This is critical to perform now because a failure to verify this functionality could lead to issues down the line. For example, if you have virtual machines that can't vMotion, that means DRS will not be able to balance your workloads appropriately. Furthermore, if you are trying to do maintenance and a running virtual machine can't be moved off the host, then it is going to be impossible to perform maintenance on that host without virtual machine downtime or resolution of the configuration problems.

You might have a cluster with mixed CPU types and will not be able to vMotion machines across the hosts without further configuration. In this case, configure Enhance vMotion Capability (EVC) to mask the host CPUs to allow for vMotion compatibility.

Verifying vMotion Network Performance

After you have verified you can vMotion any virtual machine from and to any host in the cluster, you need to make sure that vMotion operations perform to a level of performance that is deemed acceptable for your environment. Again like the testing of storage performance, this depends on your configuration, although in this case variables are much more confined. You may be using only 2-gigabit NICs without Multi-NIC vMotion or you may be using up to four 10-gigabit NICs with Multi-NIC vMotion enabled. As such, the results will vary greatly; however, following this plan allows for proper verification of vMotion network performance:

- Define a baseline. Know what to expect when just one virtual machine vMotion is performed at a time.

- Perform an individual vMotion to and from each host in your cluster.

- Perform simultaneous vMotion operations to and from various hosts in your cluster.

- Disconnect one or several NIC cables to evaluate performance during a failure.

- Use esxtop to monitor network traffic and ensure contention does not exist.

As discussed earlier, vMotion traffic is now capable of saturating a 10-gigabit link. It is likely that if you are deploying 10-gigabit CNAs, you don't have more than four of them in each server. Consider the use of Network I/O Control (NIOC) to help eliminate contention when using 10-gigabit links that are shared by traffic types other than vMotion.

When vMotion operations fail, these are the most common reasons we typically see:

- The VMkernel port did not have the vMotion check box checked.

- The CD-ROM had ISO on local storage that was not visible to the destination host.

- The virtual machine itself was located on local storage.

- CPU affinity was set on the virtual machine.

- There are inconsistent settings on the vSwitch or port group between source/destination hosts.

- There is an active connection to an internal-only vSwitch.

When vMotion operations fail to perform as expected, the most common reason is a lack of dedicated networking for vMotion. When it comes to security, we also often see the vMotion network being routed. We recommend keeping this network physically isolated or through the use of nonrouted Virtual Local Area Networks (VLAN). Also, it is important to note that vMotion operations may be taking longer than normal if you are storing VM swap files locally or on a datastore not available to all hosts. This causes vMotion operations to take longer as the swap file needs to be copied during the vMotion process.

Verifying Fault Tolerance Networking Functionality

Fault tolerance provides continuous protection for virtual machines in the event of a vSphere host failure. Whereas High Availability will restart virtual machines on another host in the event of a failure, fault tolerance ensures the virtual machine will be continuously available via a secondary copy of the virtual machine that is kept in sync with the primary.

Every operation that is performed on the primary virtual machine is repeated on the secondary virtual machine. So when you go into the machine and remove all the boot files for the operating system and reboot, you will have twice the amount of boot failures. With that said, it is not a means of providing backups and not a replacement for clustering where a single virtual machine failure cannot be tolerated.

Fault tolerance is an item that is easy to configure but requires careful thought in its design as it has implications on the design as noted:

- Requires high bandwidth network for Fault Tolerance Logging

- One vCPU maximum

- Memory reservation equal to configured memory

- DRS disabled for the protected virtual machine
- Protected machine's virtual disks must be eager zeroed thick

NOTE

A thick disk can be created as either lazy zeroed thick or eager zeroed thick. A disk that is created as lazy zeroed has all its space allocated at creation time but the blocks are not zeroed out. Eager zeroed thick allocates and zeroes out all the blocks at creation time. This leads to longer virtual machine creation times as result.

- Hosts must be processor capable and supported for FT
- Requires Enterprise or Enterprise Plus licensing

NOTE

Refer to VMware Knowledge Base (KB) article 1013428 for a complete list of considerations and requirements when using fault tolerance.

When verifying the functionality of fault tolerance, you should verify several items:

- Protecting a virtual machine
- Simulating a host failure to ensure continuous protection
- Reconfiguring protection to another host

Protecting a Virtual Machine

A failure in protecting a virtual machine can indicate a few different things. For starters, it might be as simple as configuring the Fault Tolerance Logging check box for the VMkernel port. Without a Fault Tolerance Logging Network turned on, fault tolerance for a virtual machine will fail. It might be more complex than that. Remember that fault tolerance has several limitations that exclude its use in several situations. If a virtual machine has more than one CPU, for example, the configuration will fail.

Testing the protection of a virtual machine should be a fairly easy process, but if it fails, it can be a fairly complex resolution because it will likely be the result of a miscommunication or misunderstanding during the design process. It may be the VM has a need for more than one processor. In this case, perhaps the machine might not need both CPUs configured and everything will be fine. I've seen instances, though, where fault tolerance could not be used because of an oversight during the planning of the project. In several of these cases, fault tolerance was one of the bigger, if not the biggest, functional requirements to be met. Here is one of those cases.

Case Study

You are done with the implementation and are now getting ready to verify functionality and configuration of the infrastructure over the next several days. You have verified whether High Availability, Distributed Resource Scheduling, and management networking redundancy are all properly functioning. You are ready to verify fault tolerance functionality at this point as a formality. You know it is going to work because you've configured all the hosts with dedicated Fault Tolerance Logging Networks. All the virtual machines are single-processor machines. You've even configured the disks to be eager zeroed thick virtual disks just to speed up the process.

You turn on fault tolerance on the virtual machine and to your surprise you see an error. The error states, "The Virtual Machine is running in a monitor mode that is incompatible with Fault Tolerance."

Something is not right, and after verifying your settings and trying again on several different virtual machines, it is still failing. You begin to dig deeper and notice the vSphere hosts have a lower-level CPU than was ordered and this CPU is not supported for fault tolerance. You call up the vendor to tell them the wrong CPU was sent for the hosts and the vendor tells you that was the configuration that was ordered. This can't be right—the plan was to order a configuration that included a fault-tolerant–capable CPU. After digging deeper, you find that the decision was made afterward by management to order the same model server with slightly lower specifications for CPU because of cost savings.

The packing list was checked but who would have thought that the wrong CPU could have been shipped, let alone the wrong one ordered? In the end, the project took more than a month longer to complete because of the delay. Companies with tighter budgets might not have had the flexibility to bring the servers up to spec. In this case, if fault tolerance was a design requirement, it was one that was not going to be met by the current design.

Simulating a Host Failure

If you are fortunate enough to have successfully turned on fault tolerance for one or several virtual machines, it is time to simulate a host failure. Simulating a host failure will be done to ensure the operating system and application-level continuity exists during and after the failure.

Several ways exist to force a host failure:

- Remove all networking.

- Remove all power.

- For blade servers, remove the blade.

- Force a kernel panic, the PSOD.

Verification of this test requires monitoring the operating system and application as the failover occurs as well as afterward. Simply monitoring a ping to the host and accessing the application's Web browser interface might not be enough for some environments, so planning ahead and involving the proper stakeholders is vital to testing functionality for fault tolerance and any other area for that matter.

Reprotecting a Virtual Machine

When finished, you need to reprotect the virtual machine. The process is similar to protecting the virtual machine, only this time the secondary virtual machine should be placed on a different vSphere host. This ensures the entire cluster is correctly configured and capable of supporting virtual machines configured for fault tolerance.

Verifying IP Storage Networking Functionality

Today, most virtual infrastructures deployed have some form of IP storage, whether it is NFS or iSCSI. This storage may be the primary storage for the infrastructure or it may be implemented only to store test/development or templates. Regardless, there is a need to verify whether the storage networking capabilities are functional.

This testing ends up encompassing a lot of layers, and troubleshooting issues can take the work of individuals on several teams. For example, consider the following:

- The virtual machines are running on hardware that is using gigabit or higher physical NICs to connect to physical network switches that are in some way connected to a storage device.

- This storage device in turn will have a certain storage configuration.

- It may have few or many gigabit or higher physical NICs.

- It may have disks of various speeds that are configured as various RAID types with varying amounts of LUNs on such RAID groups.

- The LUNs themselves may have varying amounts of virtual machines running on them all with distinct IOPS requirements.

In fact, it is even more complicated than mentioned. The storage will also have some varying type of cache. We also must consider the layer between the virtual machine and the physical NICs on the vSphere host. The port group in which the VMkernel port exists will have its own set of configurations that will contribute to the performance and availability of the storage to virtual machines. This certainly isn't the place to skimp on costs by reusing old Cat 5 cabling.

In terms of testing functionality, we will be looking at testing two key areas:

- Storage networking availability
- Storage networking performance

Storage Networking Availability

Similar to your testing of management networking availability earlier, you need to ensure storage networking is highly available in the event of a failover as well. You accomplish this similarly by providing redundancy in networking from the VMkernel layer all the way through to the physical network card (vmnic) and physical switch layer. Additionally, though, you might also need to configure storage failover policies.

iSCSI networking allows for the configuration of multiple VMkernel ports, and as such the storage will have configurable options for multipathing. NFS, on the other hand, is a session-based protocol that allows only a single network path from one vSphere host to one NFS server. This means that for NFS, there is no way to create multiple paths. Instead, you should create multiple VMkernel ports and multiple NFS servers on separate subnets for each NFS datastore or sets of NFS datastores.

> **NOTE**
>
> It is important to note that storage networking should be on physically separate and redundant switches. Separating out ports on an existing switch is not recommended because the resources are shared, potentially causing contention for bandwidth. Additionally, this makes it more likely that a maintenance activity to the network impacts the storage and ultimately the virtualization infrastructure.

Storage Failover NFS

Our test plan for NFS storage failover is going to be similar to that of management networking failover in that our main objective will be to verify the redundancy as there will not be storage path failover like that of iSCSI. The failover for NFS like that of management networking will be via redundant active or standby network connections from port groups that are backed by multiple vmnics. Ideally, these vmnics should be distributed to separate physical network switches. Even though NFS will only ever use one active connection, the standby network connections and secondary switches are critical if a vmnic or physical switch fails. To verify redundancy, follow this procedure:

1. Disconnect one of the vmnics that backs the VMkernel port for the NFS network being tested.

2. Verify whether NFS connectivity to the host still exists. This can be done on the host using a **vmkping** command as documented in VMware KB article 1003728.

3. Reconnect the NFS network that was disconnected.

4. Disconnect another of the vmnics that backs the VMkernel port for the NFS network being tested.

5. Verify whether NFS connectivity still exists to the host.

6. Reconnect the NFS network that was disconnected.

NOTE

To sidestep for a minute, let's talk about the **vmkping** command and why we don't issue just the **ping** command. The **vmkping** command will source the request using the server's VMkernel port. If we used the **ping** command, we would be testing connectivity from the server's management network to the NFS server's IP address. We do not recommend it, but the NFS network may be routed. If this were the case, then this would result in a successful ping test, even though we haven't actually checked whether the server can truly access the NFS server via its VMkernel port.

Storage Failover iSCSI

The use of iSCSI provides some unique options for multipathing and load balancing not available to NFS. For redundancy, we recommend configuring iSCSI port binding using multiple VMkernel ports backed by separate vmnics. When used with the Round Robin path selection policy, this provides the greatest benefits in terms of redundancy and load balancing. Additionally, it is highly recommended that separate physical network switches dedicated for iSCSI traffic be used.

When configuring iSCSI port binding, you must consider the following:

- You must configure multiple VMkernel ports.

- Each VMkernel port should be backed by a unique active NIC and only one active NIC.

- Vendor requirements may dictate your configuration. For example, port binding with the EMC Clariion requires VMkernel ports in different subnets.

Although this used to be a process that could be done only via the command line, vSphere 5 has now introduced the ability to bind VMkernel ports through the graphical user interface (GUI). For more detailed information on configuring iSCSI port binding, refer to the *vSphere Storage Guide* (see Appendix A).

To verify redundancy of iSCSI port binding, you may do the following:

1. Disconnect one of the vmnics that backs one of the VMkernel ports for the iSCSI network being tested.

2. Verify whether connectivity to the host still exists.

3. Reconnect the network that was disconnected.

4. Disconnect another of the vmnics that backs the VMkernel port for the iSCSI network being tested.

5. Verify whether connectivity to the host still exists.

6. Reconnect the network that was disconnected.

To verify iSCSI multipathing is functioning, complete the following steps:

1. Launch esxtop.

2. Press the **n** key to enter the networking view.

3. Perform a storage vMotion involving a datastore on your iSCSI network.

4. Monitor the Packet Transmits (PKTTX/s) for activity. You will be looking for activity on all the VMkernel ports that were bound for the initiator, as highlighted in Figure 2.5.

```
192.168.1.41 - PuTTY                                                    _ 6 X
7:27:38pm up  1:06, 311 worlds, 1 VMs, 1 vCPUs; CPU load average: 0.02, 0.02, 0.02

  PORT-ID          USED-BY  TEAM-PNIC DNAME         PKTTX/s  MbTX/s  PKTRX/s
  16777217      Management        n/a vSwitch0         0.00    0.00     0.00
  16777218         vmnic0          - vSwitch0         33.30    0.45    19.25
  16777219         vmnic1          - vSwitch0          6.69    0.00    29.83
  16777220           vmk0    vmnic0 vSwitch0          32.47    0.45    11.19
  16777221           vmk1    vmnic0 vSwitch0           2.20    0.00     9.29
  16777222           vmk2    vmnic1 vSwitch0           6.69    0.00    28.57
  16777223     3673:vnx01    vmnic1 vSwitch0           0.00    0.00     2.56
  16777224     3673:vnx01    vmnic0 vSwitch0           2.00    0.00     4.46
  16777225     3673:vnx01    vmnic0 vSwitch0           0.00    0.00     2.56
```

Figure 2.5   Verifying iSCSI Multipathing

On the vSphere side, you have now verified the network failover redundancy, but let's take a moment to talk about some things you haven't verified by doing so. You haven't verified whether the network switches themselves are ready for a failover event. You also have not verified whether there is true redundancy on the storage side. You might know that four physical network connections go into the storage split among multiple switches, but at this point, you have not verified the storage will function in the event of failure to one or more of those network connections. Networking connectivity to storage is often itself virtualized, so there is a lot to consider when testing and troubleshooting performance and connectivity issues with IP-based storage.

Fully testing the redundancy of your storage or network will vary based on your configuration and vendor; however, we suggest at a minimum you power off redundant physical switches and fail back and forth among them. Additionally, we suggest removing storage controller cabling and inducing failover and failback of LUNs presented to storage processors.

Storage Redundancy and Failback

We previously discussed IP storage functionality testing, and it is now time to focus on Fibre Channel networking functionality specifically. You may have a 2-, 4-, or 8Gbps Fibre Channel infrastructure and you will have a varying amount of storage processors, disks, raid types, LUNs, and virtual machines running on those storage devices. You can reference the previous section on IP storage performance testing, which is the same in terms of the execution; however, the expectations vary, so keep the considerations of your configuration in mind when you lay out your performance testing.

When looking at storage redundancy, your testing will mimic that of the iSCSI redundancy. Similar to iSCSI redundancy testing, you also need to test the redundancy of the storage and networking itself by failing over LUNs to the other storage processor where applicable. Although iSCSI is dependent upon network switching and the proper setup of traditional IP networking, Fibre Channel storage is dependent upon proper zoning of hosts and masking of LUNs to work effectively. This must be done correctly for all storage processors for failover to work correctly. Your environment will ideally have hosts with multiple HBAs connected to two separate fabrics, which in turn are connected to storage with multiple storage processors. This might not always be possible, so your testing can vary. To verify Fibre Channel storage redundancy from vSphere, follow these steps:

1. Disconnect one of the HBAs.

2. Verify whether connectivity to the host still exists.

3. Reconnect the HBA that was disconnected.

4. Disconnect another HBA.

5. Verify whether connectivity to the host still exists.

6. Reconnect the HBA that was disconnected.

You also need to test the failover by performing the following:

1. From your storage device, failover LUNs to another storage processor.

2. Disconnect paths from your storage device.

3. Disconnect one of the fabrics, where multiple fabrics exist.

4. Disconnect paths from your vSphere hosts.

You might also want to remove power to a storage processor or from redundant switching to test what will occur during a failure of either of these components.

PowerPath/VE

This is a good time to briefly mention another option for managing paths that will provide for the greatest benefits in terms of throughput and failover. PowerPath/VE provides dynamic load balancing and failover for virtual environments. It also works to continually ensure paths are optimized. An in-depth discussion of PowerPath is beyond the scope of this book; however, you can find more information on PowerPath and the best practices for using it in your vSphere environment in Appendix A.

Storage Networking Performance

Developing a test plan for storage performance involves a firm understanding of the individual infrastructure that has been rolled out. We expect very different results for the performance of NFS storage running over gigabit connectivity that is backed by 10K SATA drives than NFS storage running over 10-gigabit connectivity that is backed by 15K SATA drives. Regardless, a standard methodology can be followed that allows the testing of the storage that you have deployed. You just need to make sure you have a baseline developed beforehand with your environment's expectations. In addition, you should be seeking to define a baseline going forward for storage performance expectations.

You should look at a few different areas of storage performance. For starters, you need to look at the overall performance of the storage for virtual machine operation. Second, you need to look at performance during actions such as rebalancing of datastores using storage vMotion.

When looking at storage performance for virtual machine operation, you can accomplish this at one of three layers:

- At the Virtual Machine layer
- At the Host layer
- At the Storage layer

You can measure performance by looking at the performance statistics of each individual virtual machine. You can do this by looking at each virtual machine and gauging performance by looking at the performance of guest operating systems. You can use tools such as Perfmon in Windows or top in Linux to see what the performance is from the perspective of the guest. You also can use tools like IOMeter to stress test the storage and see what your disk throughput is.

You also can measure performance at the Host layer. This can be done by using esxtop to check disk metrics for each host. If you are not familiar with esxtop, check out Appendix A for further resources. You can additionally check out VMware KB article 1008205, which describes the use of esxtop for troubleshooting performance issues (also see Appendix A for a link to said article).

Finally, you can measure performance at the Storage layer. This varies from vendor to vendor, but your storage vendor should have several interfaces and tools that allow historical and real-time monitoring of the storage performance.

In addition to looking at storage networking performance for normal operations, you need to test during one and several Storage vMotion operations. Again, the testing can take place in one or all of the layers. When testing, you are looking to define a baseline for future performance expectations.

Quality Assurance Assessment

Quality assurance can mean different things to different people, so let's start by defining what *we* mean by quality assurance verification for vSphere environments.

During the quality assurance assessment, you are looking to verify your implementation matches its intended configuration. This configuration is detailed in the design documentation but may have been overlooked or incorrectly input during the implementation. If there have been no changes in configuration due to a change in requirements, the configuration must match exactly. Checking functionality does not reveal all errors in configuration. Items may be fully functional, but when not configured correctly, could cause issues later on or provide less-than-optimal performance.

Automation should be used where possible to avoid inconsistencies and human error. Whether automation has been used or not, configuration errors are possible. Similar to the test for functionality, a quality assurance checklist should be created and maintained for current versions of vSphere.

The following sections describe some of the configuration items you should verify and some tools for helping the process.

VMware vSphere Health Check Delivery

The VMware vSphere health check is a paid engagement delivered by either VMware or an authorized solution provider of VMware. During this engagement, data is collected using the Health Check tool and analyzed to provide a report. This report is delivered to the customer along with guidance on resolving issues and concerns that have been found. When it comes to verifying configuration and compliance with generally accepted best practices and norms, the money spent toward a Health Check is well worth it. Areas are found where the configuration is not optimal, which assists in finding areas for remediation. Items are also uncovered that might not be configured as you originally intended or might be inconsistent between hosts in a cluster. Health Checks are typically done for an existing environment that has been running for some time, but immediately after an implementation is a great time for them as well.

As a VMware authorized solution provider, we can attest firsthand to the benefits of the Health Check delivery.

You are guaranteed to have someone who is a VMware Certified Professional (VCP) or above.

Individuals performing and delivering the Health Check engagements have performed these engagements across many different organizations and, as a result, have a level of experience that has exposed them to the common misconfigurations found in vSphere deployments.

We have performed many health checks, and there are clear trends in some of the items that are commonly misconfigured. Throughout this book, we provide you with many of these common pitfalls along with guidance on remediating your environment.

VMware vSphere Health Check Script

If you prefer to run a health check yourself, a great community resource is available that allows for a daily email to be sent with a nicely configured report. This provides for a nice and simple view of your environment and shows off not just configuration items, but performance information as well. More resources on this script and implementing it can be found in Appendix A.

Verifying Configurations

Many configurations could be made into an infrastructure, and it would be impossible to discuss them all. There are, however, several common misconfigurations we encounter that occur either during the implementation phase or are changed afterward. In some cases, these may be items that are the defaults and should be changed and in others are simply misconfigured.

vCenter Specific Configurations

The following settings are focused on configuration items on the vCenter server:

- **HA Admission Control Policy not configured as intended**—If a mistake is made in configuring the HA Admission Control Policy, an issue almost never occurs immediately. However, two things can happen later. First, the cluster might not allow the powering on of additional virtual machines to a quantity that was previously expected. Second, in situations with mixed configuration hosts, a certain host failure could lead to a situation where not all the virtual machines can continue to run safely or in an optimal fashion.

- **DRS not configured as intended**—A failure to enable DRS or configure it correctly is common. Not enabling leads to no rebalancing of your hosts during resource contention. Misconfiguring may lead to either too many migrations or very few migrations occurring.

- **vCenter server configured below minimum specifications**—This is more than just how you have configured the vCenter server but also what other pieces you are choosing to install on that server. In some smaller environments, SQL may be installed on the same box along with Update Manager. If you accidentally configured the vCenter server with only one CPU and only 2GB of RAM, you will soon realize the need to increase these configurations.

- **Database server not configured correctly**—The database server configuration is an area that is often overlooked. I rarely run in to a VMware administrator who was or is a database administrator, so this should come as no surprise. It is not uncommon to see any of the following issues with the database server:

  - Disks backing the server are not sufficient for the database.

  - The database is on the same volume as the operating system, Update Manager database, or other software that can lead to contention and volumes filling up.

  - Database cleanup tasks are not configured correctly and regular maintenance fails to occur. This leads to poor performing databases and the potential to fill up volumes and halt the database.

- **DNS servers not specified correctly**—If you input the DNS servers wrong, you might not immediately notice any issues. However, once you try to use Update Manager, you will soon realize the DNS servers are not correctly configured.

- **ESXi added to vCenter by IP address**—We've seen many times where hosts are added to vCenter by IP address. Hosts should be added to DNS and then added by hostname to avoid any potential issues with High Availability or Update Manager.

- **Incorrectly configured resource reservations and limits**—This can be resource pools, specific reservations, or limits. It can be in the form of CPU and memory, or network and storage. Regardless, a failure to properly execute the configuration of any resource reservations or limits can lead to drastic resource issues in your infrastructure.

- **Not configuring syslog**—We often find that a syslog server is either incorrectly configured or not configured at all. In an environment without a syslog server, there are other alternatives. With ESXi being stateless and not retaining the logs upon a reboot, it is critical to ship the logs somewhere in the event of an issue. It is not often that I hear of a vSphere host crash; however, it is not uncommon to speak to someone who is having issues and rebooted his or her host as part of trouble-shooting. Important historical information about the issue will not be present if the logs are not shipped somewhere else.

Our recommendation is to install a syslog server. They are very handy for not just your virtual infrastructure but for all of your networking devices as well. Furthermore, vCenter now ships with a syslog server that can be installed from the vCenter media, as shown in Figure 2.6. Additionally, the vSphere Management Assistant (vMA) also allows for syslog collection and has for some time now.

If this is not feasible, you can also change the log directory and redirect the logs to another datastore. If you point this to a centralized datastore location, you will have all of your log files in one location. Alternatively, if you want to use some of that unused local datastore space to store your logs, they will persist even after a reboot. To do this, you need to go to each host and do the following:

1. On the Configuration tab, choose Advanced Settings under the Software section.

2. Browse to Syslog in the left pane.

3. Change Syslog.global.logdir to a path on the host's local datastore.

4. You must properly format the datastore name by typing it between the two brackets:

```
[vmfs01-raid1-data] /logs/vspherehost01
```

Figure 2.6   VMware Syslog Collector

Host-Specific Configurations

Now that we have discussed some vCenter configuration issues, let's move on to the hosts themselves. The following settings or configurations are focused on vSphere hosts themselves, including not only the vSphere software but also the underlying hardware and connectivity at the host level:

- **Host hardware not configured correctly or optimally**—For starters, it is recommended to install your vendor's specific customized ISO if available. A failure to do so can lead to issues such as the following:

  - Information missing under Hardware Status due to lack of CIM provider

  - Less-than-optimal hardware performance

  Additionally, these other items often are not correctly configured:

  - Up-to-date host BIOS and hardware firmware. Without disregarding VMware's Hardware Compatibility List, you need to ensure that the host BIOS and hardware firmware are up to date across not only the server hardware but also the networking and storage environment. This tool can be accessed online by going to http://vmware.com/go/hcl.

  - If your hardware is NUMA capable, you must disable node interleaving in the BIOS.

- If your hardware supports hyperthreading, enable it.

- PCI devices not placed consistently across hosts in a cluster.

- **vSphere not configured correctly on host**—These are several common configuration items we find that should be corrected:

  - Different versions of vSphere installed on hosts in the same cluster. This often does not cause any issues; however, it is not recommended.

  - Failure to stop technical support mode or SSH after usage.

  - Failure to properly configure Network Time Protocol (NTP). This is often set up; however, many forget to make sure it is set to start up automatically.

  - Inconsistency in configurations host-to-host in the cluster. This can lead to confusion when administering as well as issues with vMotion and other critical features of vSphere.

  - Inconsistent Path Selection Plugin (PSP) and primary paths between hosts in a cluster.

Virtual Machine–Specific Configurations

The following settings or configurations are focused on virtual machine–specific configuration items:

- VMs have ISOs attached on nonshared storage or they are located on nonshared storage.

- VMs have snapshots taken during initial rollout that have not been removed.

- VMs that have been migrated from a physical server using P2V converter or another tool have hardware that is no longer needed, such as communication ports or floppy drives.

- Although not specifically a configuration item, it is important to remember to make sure snapshots are removed after an initial rollout if they were created. A failure to do so could lead to issues later on. PowerShell is a great tool to check for the existence of snapshots in your cluster.

- Virtual machine has leftover software for hardware-specific functionality after P2V conversion. A server that used to be physical will have lots of software that is no longer needed. This eats up resources, so removing this software is highly recommended.

▪ Virtual machine was not properly resized after P2V conversion. Rarely, a virtual machine should be configured exactly identical to its existing configuration. When this occurs, it is usually to ensure there are no issues as a result of changes to these items on top of migrating to a virtual server. During the migration process, you have the option to change not only CPU or memory, but also contract or expand drives in the process. For CPU and memory, start small and scale up unless the operating system or application specifically requires it. For disk space, ensure you have enough for the present plus room to grow, but don't carry over a 1TB operating system drive just because the physical server had it.

Storage Configurations

Proper storage configuration is going to be heavily reliant on the best practices and configurations recommended by your storage provider. There are, however, many areas in which configuration errors commonly occur, outside of vendor-specific configurations:

▪ **Storage firmware and updates**—Your storage vendor will have bugs and fixes just like any other hardware and operating system. As a result, you need to pay close attention when implementing that the storage is at a firmware level that is currently supported. Additionally, you need to make sure your host's HBAs are also up to date and in line with your storage vendor's recommendations.

▪ **Failure to properly configure multipathing**—A failure to properly configure multipathing leads to unexpected results if a storage path goes down. If you are also deploying load balancing, your storage might not be sending traffic down multiple paths at the same time.

▪ **Storage vendor recommendations**—Pay close attention to any recommendations made by your storage vendor. For example, you need to make any recommended changes to the queue depth settings on the HBAs. Additionally, depending on the type of storage, you need to ensure the recommended path selection policy is selected.

▪ **Failure to properly size datastores**—If you create many smaller datastores, you will likely have much more wasted space than if you had several larger datastores. However, the larger the datastore, the more virtual machines that will be running and the greater the chance that you will experience contention for disk resources. The primary performance issue we see in virtualization environments is storage performance as a result of the lack of disk spindle count.

▪ **Failure to redirect swap files**—If you are using VMware's Site Recovery Manager (SRM), the solution might have been designed around storing the swap files on separate datastores that would not be replicated. Failing to properly implement this leads to a large amount of data that will be replicated. If the links between the two sites are not sufficient, this can cause some issues and a failure to meet recovery point objectives.

Network Configurations

Proper network configuration ensures your infrastructure's networking performs well during normal operation and continues to function properly during a failure. The following are key areas we often find incorrectly configured:

- **Failure to configure portfast**—A failure to configure portfast on the switch can lead to issues if a spanning tree loop is detected during convergence. To configure portfast on a Cisco switch, you must enter Configuration mode and enter the command **spanning-tree portfast** for an access port or **spanning-tree portfast trunk** for a trunk port. For Nexus switches, enter **spanning-tree portfast type edge trunk**. For more information on portfast, refer to the VMware KB article 1003804 (a link is provided in Appendix A).

- **Failure to adjust default security settings**—By default, the security for a vSwitch is not set to what is recommended. Both options for MAC address changes and forged transmits are set to Accept. For security reasons, unless these are needed, they should be set to Reject for all vSwitches.

- **Failure to configure auto-negotiation for vmnics**—Although everything may work fine with networking configured as Gb/full or 10Gb/full, there are known issues by doing so:

  - In certain cases, performance is degraded when auto-negotiation does not take place. Some non-Cisco devices support the use of half-duplex Gigabit.

  - If flow control is desired, you cannot statically configure your network adapters; they must be negotiated.

  For more information on why auto-negotiation is recommended, refer to VMware KB article 1004089 (a link is provided in Appendix A).

- **Lack of networking redundancy**—In some cases, I've seen the order of network adapter port numbers differ from that of the vmnics. In other cases, it turned out they were hooked up in the wrong location. Either way, the result was a lack of redundancy against failure that was originally planned for. This can happen when virtual machine port groups are set up with certain active or standby NICs in a manner that provides redundancy across separate physical switches and via separate network interface cards. What can result are both NICs from a particular port group traversing the same switch.

This type of configuration issue might be noticed immediately if some of the ports are configured as access ports. Hooking into the wrong access port causes you to quickly notice a lack of network connectivity for one of your services, but if they are all trunk ports with the same VLANs being trunked, then there won't be any connectivity or functionality issues.

Implementing the Solution Summary

This chapter focused on the implementation phase of virtualization projects. This phase of the project requires taking a design and translating it into a working infrastructure. A design blueprint is a critical prerequisite to this phase and provides for the greatest success of the implementation in terms of the quality. Even with a well-outlined design in terms of a design blueprint, issues do occur.

It is, then, those decisions about how to tackle those issues that are of utmost importance.

The responsibility of the implementer is not simply translating a design blueprint into a fully implemented virtualization solution. As the implementer, you should review the work of the design laid out and ensure all the pieces of the puzzle are still there and as they were when the design was scoped out. Don't assume anything.

Furthermore, as the implementer, you should question decisions made in the design where necessary. Although it might not be likely best practices are going to be violated, it is very possible solutions will be designed that fail to consider pieces of information that were not known at the time of the design.

In some environments, the infrastructure might never be touched again for months at a time. This is the beauty of VMware and its feature set, including HA and DRS. A host could lose power and virtual machines may begin to contend with each other. If everything is designed and implemented to plan properly, though, there is not a need to manually administer anything. Always implement with this type of self-sufficiency in mind and you will continue laying a solid foundation for the organization's infrastructure.

Chapter 3

Operating the Environment

This chapter focuses on maintaining and monitoring an active environment. At this point, you might or might not have designed an optimal environment. The environment also might not have been implemented to your standards. After all, sometimes you can't entirely fix what is currently broken and must deal with it for a period of time.

In the field, we see the excitement in customers' eyes at the power that VMware brings to their infrastructures. Cost savings through hardware, high availability, and ease of management are the main things they are eager to take advantage of. However, this excitement sometimes leads to a lack of focus on some of the new things that must be considered with a virtual infrastructure. A lack of maintenance and insufficient or no monitoring are two huge issues that must be considered. Before delving into maintaining and monitoring a virtual infrastructure, this chapter talks about some other operational items that you might not have considered in the design.

Backups

A virtual infrastructure can pose different challenges for backups in terms of a technical understanding of the environment. This is the main reason we see that backups are not being adequately performed. Every organization has its own set of requirements for backups, but consider the following as important items for a backup strategy:

- An appropriate recovery point objective (RPO) or the ability to roll back to a period of time from today

- An appropriate retention policy, or the number of copies of previous periods of times retained

- An appropriate recovery time objective (RTO) or the ability to restore the appropriate backups in a set time

- An appropriate location of both onsite and offsite backups to enable recovery of data in the event of a complete disaster, while still allowing for a quick restore onsite where needed

- The ability to properly verify the validity of your backup infrastructure through regular testing and verification

Furthermore, outside of a technical understanding of the virtual infrastructure, virtualization poses no other significant challenges to maintaining a backup strategy. In fact, it will actually enable easier and quicker restores if properly designed.

When considering your backup strategy, you need to consider your RTO and RPO. You also need to consider your retention policy and proper offsite storage of backups. Properly storing offsite copies of backups is not just about keeping copies offsite that allow a quick restore to a recent restore point. It is also about considering what to also keep onsite so that simple restores are just that. Beyond that, you need to make sure you have all the small details that make up your infrastructure. This includes credentials, phone numbers for individuals and vendors, documentation, and redundancy in each of these contacts and documentation locations.

When considering backups, you need to determine the proper mix of file-level backups or virtual machine–level backups. Some organizations continue to do backups from within the guest that can provide a bare-metal restore. This is still a good option, and it might be your only option because of the software you presently use for backups; however, it will not be as quick to restore as a backup product that uses the VMware vStorage APIs to provide a complete virtual machine restore.

Let's take a moment to talk about the verification and monitoring of your backups. Taking backups is not the solution to the task of creating a backup strategy. The solution is the ability to restore the missing or corrupted data to a point in time and within a certain time as dictated by your businesses requirements. Therefore, it is always important to regularly test restoration practices and abilities as well as monitor for issues with backup jobs. Your backup product should be able to verify the data was backed up and not corrupted; however, you should also schedule regular tests to verify this.

And, finally, let's talk about snapshots. Snapshots are not backups, but in some environments they are used in that fashion. Snapshots are useful when performing updates on a virtual machine as a means of quick rollback; however, they should not be used long term. We've witnessed two main things that occur as a result of snapshots being left behind.

For starters, they result in data needing to be written multiple times. If you have three snapshots, any new data is written to all three. As you can see in Figure 3.1, blocks of data that need to be written are written to each snapshot file, resulting in a performance hit as well as increased space utilization. Multiply this by several virtual machines and possibly even worse by multiple nested snapshots, and it is no wonder that we see datastores fill up because of old snapshots. This can bring virtual machines to their knees and makes rectifying the situation complex. When consolidating snapshots, you need to have space available to write the data to the original virtual machine disk. In this case, you would not have that available, requiring the migration of virtual machines to other datastores.

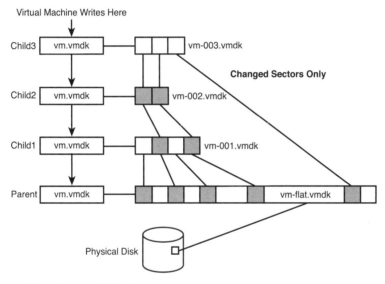

Figure 3.1 Snapshot Disk Chain

A second problem we have seen many times is often caused by full datastores. Snapshot corruption can occur as a result, leading to the disappearance of any data since the time of the snapshot creation. For example, assume a single snapshot was taken six months ago, right after you installed Windows for your new Exchange server. If that snapshot is corrupted, you will likely be able to repoint to the original VMware Disk (VMDK) file; however, you'll be left with a bare Windows virtual machine. Full datastores are not the only time snapshots can be corrupted. This can also occur as a result of problems during snapshot consolidation or manipulating the original virtual machine disk file from the command line while snapshots are present.

It is important to note that a snapshot itself contains only the changes that occur after the snapshot was taken. If the original virtual machine disk is corrupted, you will lose all of your data. Snapshots are dependent on the virtual machine disk.

VMware's Knowledge Base (KB) article 1025279 discusses in detail the best practices when using snapshots. In general, we recommend using snapshots only as needed and for short periods of time. We recommend configuring alarms within vCenter to notify of snapshot creation and regularly checking for snapshots in your environment. There are many PowerShell scripts available that will accomplish this; however, a great tool to have that includes snapshot reporting is PowerGUI (see Appendix A, "Additional Resources," for reference).

Within vCenter, no default alarms exist to alarm for snapshots. You can, however, create a virtual machine alarm with the following trigger to alarm for snapshots, as shown in Figure 3.2. This will help you with snapshots that have been left behind for some time and have grown to 1GB or larger; however, it will not help until the total amount of snapshot data written for a virtual machine totals 1GB. This chapter discusses alarms later, but you can also check out VMware Knowledge Base article 1018029 for a detailed video demonstration of creating an alarm like this one (see Appendix A for a link).

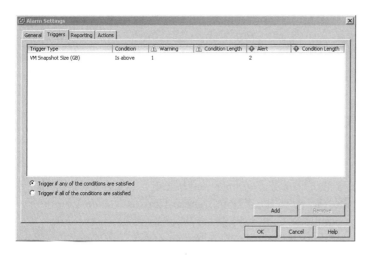

Figure 3.2 Configuring Snapshot Alarms

Data Recovery

Like many products that use the VMware vStorage APIs, VMware's Data Recovery provides the ability to overcome backup windows. That is not to say you might not want to consider backup windows because you also must consider the traffic that will occur on the network during backups; however, backup windows are of less concern for a few reasons. For starters, Data Recovery provides block-based deduplication and only copies the incremental changes. This occurs from a snapshot copy of the virtual machine that enables virtual machines to continue running while Data Recovery performs the backup from that snapshot copy.

Data Recovery is not going to be the end-all solution to your backup strategy, though. Its intention is to provide disk-based backup storage for your local storage and there is not a native method built in to transfer these backups to tape or other media. Therefore, VMware Data Recovery is best thought of as a complementing product to an existing backup infrastructure. With that said, let's talk about some of the capabilities the product has.

The process to get backups up and running is straightforward:

- Install Data Recovery.
- Define a shared repository location.
- Define a backup job.

Installing Data Recovery

The first thing you need to verify is whether the product will meet your needs. Some of the more common things to consider when implementing Data Recovery are as follows:

- As previously mentioned, Data Recovery is intended to provide a quick method for onsite restores and does not provide offsite capabilities.
- Furthermore, you need to be sure all of your hosts are running ESX or ESXi 4.0 or later.
- Make note that each appliance supports 100 virtual machines with eight simultaneous backups. There is also a maximum of ten appliances per vCenter installation.
- The deduplication store requires a minimum of 10GB of free disk space. When using CIFS, the maximum supported size is 500GB. When using RDM or VMDK deduplication stores, the maximum supported size is 1TB.
- There is a maximum of two deduplication stores per backup appliance.
- Data Recovery will not protect machines with fault tolerance (FT) enabled or virtual machines disks that are marked as Independent.

For a complete list of supported configurations, refer to the *VMware Data Recovery Administration Guide*.

There are two steps to get the appliance installed. First, install the vSphere Client plug-in. Second, import the OVF, which will guide you through where you want to place the appliance. Once completed, you might want to consider adding an additional hard disk, which can be used to store backups.

Defining a Shared Repository

As discussed, each appliance will be limited to two shared repositories and depending on the type of repository, you will be limited to either 500GB (CIFS) or 1TB (virtual hard disk or RDM). You have the following options when choosing to define a shared repository:

- Create an additional virtual hard drive (1TB or less).
- Create a CIFS repository (500GB or less).
- Use a RDM (1TB or less).

If you choose to create and attach an additional virtual hard disk, you need to consider where you are placing it. As mentioned previously, the intention of Data Recovery is to deliver the capability of a quick onsite restore. The use of virtual hard drives provides for the best possible performance. If you use a virtual hard disk, though, you will be storing the backups within the environment they are protecting, so you must consider this carefully. You could store the virtual hard disk on the plentiful local storage that may be present on one of the hosts. You could also store the virtual hard disk on any IP-based or Fibre Channel datastore.

Our recommendation in this case is to use the local storage of one of the hosts if it is available. When given the choice between the two, consider the likelihood of your shared storage failing versus the local storage of a server failing. Additionally, consider the repercussion of each of those failing. If your shared storage were to fail with the backups on them, you would have to use your other backup infrastructure to restore them, which can be quite time consuming. If the local server with your backups on them were to fail, then if a complete disaster occurs you are still going to have the production copies running on shared storage. If you do have a complete site failure, then you are going to need to deploy your disaster recovery strategy. This is discussed further shortly.

Another option is to use a Raw Device Mapping (RDM). If you are using the same storage as your virtual infrastructure, you are taking the same risks. The only way to mitigate such risks is to use storage dedicated for the purposes of backups. Just like the option of using virtual disks, think about where you are going to restore that data to if a disaster occurs. If your storage device is gone, you are going to have to initiate your disaster recovery strategy.

Another option is to use a CIFS share. Remember that CIFS shares are limited to 500GB, so each appliance can only support 1TB of CIFS repositories with its two-repository limit. Although the product lets you configure a CIFS share greater than 500GB, it warns you not to do so. We recommend that you listen to the warning because testing of the product has proven that creating a large CIFS repository can cause Data Recovery to fail to finish its integrity checking, which in turn causes backups to not run.

Another consideration for CIFS is that the share you are sharing out, and for that matter the disk that is being used, should not be used for any other function. Remember that Data Recovery provides for block-based data deduplication. If other data exists on the back-end disk, this can also cause a failure in integrity checking and, in turn, a failure of backup jobs running.

Defining a Backup Job

Now that the appliance is set up and you have set up one or two repositories, it is time to create the backup jobs. Backup jobs entail choosing the following:

- Which virtual machines will be backed up
- The backup destination
- The backup window
- The retention policy

Choosing Which Virtual Machines to Back Up

The virtual machines you choose to back up can be defined by an individual virtual machine level or from vCenter, datacenter, cluster, folder, or resource pool levels as well. Note that when you choose a virtual machine based on the entity it is in, if it is moved it will no longer be backed up by that job.

Choosing a Backup Destination

Your choice of a destination might or might not matter based on the size of your infrastructure or your backup strategy. For sizing purposes, consider that you could exceed the capacity of the deduplication store if you put too many virtual machines on the same destination. For purposes of restoring data, consider the placement of the backups and where it is in your infrastructure.

Defining a Backup Window

Backup windows dictate when the jobs are allowed to run; however, they do not have a direct correlation to the exact time they will execute. By default, jobs are set from 6:00

a.m. to 6:00 p.m. Monday through Friday and all day Saturday and Sunday. Consider staggering the jobs so that multiple jobs do not run simultaneously if you are concerned with network throughput.

Defining a Retention Policy

When choosing a retention policy, you have the option of few, more, many, or custom. Custom allows specifying the retention of as many recent and older backups as required. The other options have their defaults set, as shown in Table 3.1.

Table 3.1   VMware Data Recovery Retention Policies

Retention Policy	Recent Backups	Weekly	Monthly	Quarterly	Yearly
Few	7	4	3	0	0
More	7	8	6	4	1
Many	15	8	3	8	3

Changing any one of the settings for these policies will result in the use of a custom policy. When choosing your retention policy, ensure you have the capability to restore data from as far back as you need, but within the confines of the storage you have to use for backups.

At this point, your backups are up and running. You can either initiate a backup now or wait until the backup window has been entered for backups to begin. Once you've seen your first successful backup, you still have a few other items to consider.

Restoring Data (Full, File, Disks) Verification

When restoring data, you have two key things to consider. When choosing to restore data, you first need to choose your source. A virtual machine can be part of multiple backup jobs, so in addition to having a different set of restore points, you might also have a set of restore points that are also located on a different backup repository. Second, you need to consider where you want to restore the data.

For the purposes of testing the capability to restore, you can perform a restore rehearsal by doing the following from within the Data Recovery interface by right-clicking a virtual machine and then clicking the Restore Rehearsal from Last Backup option. To fully test a restore or to perform an actual restore, you have much more to consider because this option chooses the most recent restore and restores the virtual machine without networking attached. The following sections discuss those considerations further.

Choosing Backup Source

When restoring, you have the option to restore at any level in the tree, so you can restore entire clusters, datacenters, folders, resource pools, or everything under a vCenter server. When looking at the restore of an individual virtual machine, you can restore the entire virtual machine or just specific virtual disks. You may also restore individual virtual machines from the virtual machine backup, which is discussed shortly.

Choosing Restore Destination

When restoring, you have several options during the restore, including choosing where to restore the data. When considering restoring an entire virtual machine, you have the following options to consider:

- Restore the VM to a specific datastore.

- Restore the virtual disk(s) to a specific datastore(s).

- Restore the virtual disk(s) and attach to another virtual machine.

- Choose the Virtual Disk Node.

- Restore the VM configuration (yes/no).

- Reconnect the NIC (yes/no).

When restoring, the default setting is to restore the virtual disk in place, so be careful to consider this if it is your intended result. If possible, in all situations you should restore to another location to retain the set of files that is currently in place if further restore efforts are needed on those files.

File Level Restores

In addition to restoring complete virtual machines or specific disks, you may also restore individual files. File Level Restore (FLR) allows for individual file restoration with an in-guest installed software component. The FLR client is available for both Windows and Linux guests and must be copied off the Data Recovery media locally where it will run. By default, Data Recovery only allows the restoration for files from a virtual machine for which the client is being run; however, if you run the client in Advanced mode, you can restore files from any of the virtual machines being backed up. Note that although you are able to mount Linux or Windows virtual machines regardless of the operating system you are running, you might not be able to read the volumes themselves.

Once mounted, you have the ability to copy files and restore them to locations manually or look through them to find the version you are looking for. The mounted copies are read-only versions of the files, and any changes made will not be saved, so make sure to copy the files to a desired location before making any changes.

One last note on the use of FLR when using Data Recovery: It is not recommended and Data Recovery should be configured so that File Level Restores are not possible. This is done by configuring the VMware Data Recovery .ini file and setting EnableFileRestore to 0.

Site Disaster

As mentioned previously, the intended use of this product is for quick restores and is not intended to be your disaster recovery plan. If you were to lose a vCenter server and needed to recover another machine, you would have to stand up a new vCenter server and install the plug-in to use Data Recovery to restore the virtual machine. Additionally, if you lose the appliance itself, you must install a new one and import the repository. Be aware that this can take a long time if a full integrity check is required.

Monitoring Backup Jobs

Data Recovery allows the configuration of an email notification that can be sent as often as once a day at a specified time. There isn't much to configure with email notification, as shown in Figure 3.3. The important thing is to make sure the appropriate individuals are being notified and that mail is being relayed from the outgoing mail server specified. Remember the server that needs to be authorized is not the vCenter server but rather the Data Recovery appliance itself.

Figure 3.3   Configuring Data Recovery Email Notifications

Managing the Data Recovery Repository

The maintenance tasks that run will check the integrity of the data in the repositories and reclaim space in the deduplication stores. By default, Data Recovery is set to be able to run maintenance at any time. This might not be a problem for your environment; however, when integrity check operations are occurring, backups cannot. Therefore, you should change the maintenance window so that it is set to run during a specified period of time. This ensures backups will always have the time to run each day.

When the deduplication store is using less than 80% of the repository, the retention policy is checked weekly to remove any restore points that are outside the specifications. This means that you might have many more restore points than expected as a result. Once 80% of the repository is utilized, the retention policy is checked daily. In the case of the repository filling up, the retention policy is run immediately if it has not been executed in the last 12 hours.

Disaster Recovery

Disaster recovery is an area of many organizations that has at least some, if not a lot, of room for improvement. When looking at a disaster recovery plan, the following things are important to consider:

- Data is available with an RTO that meets the business's requirements to operate and the data is from a point in time that meets the RPO of the organization.

- Data has been verified as being valid.

- A runbook has been defined for how to and in what order to restore.

The first point is present in most organizations, whereas the second and third are not. It should not be surprising because a failure warranting declaring a disaster is not often needed. Nonetheless, a solid runbook should be defined for your infrastructure. A runbook for restoration for your virtual infrastructure is crucial; however, consider the back-end networking infrastructure first as your virtual machines will be of no use without it.

When looking at recovering your virtual infrastructure, the ideal setup is to replicate among your storage devices and use VMware's Site Recovery Manager (SRM) to automate your restore. Site Recovery Manager is further discussed later in this chapter; however, for those not familiar, it assists in automating the recovery of virtual machine environments during a disaster.

You may also use the set of replicated data to manually configure the virtual machines and power them on at your disaster recovery location. Additionally, you can choose another method of manual restoration. This could be using a copy of the virtual machine files from some other mechanism or using a backup product to perform a bare-metal copy of the machine and restoring it to a newly configured virtual machine. For the purposes of this discussion, we talk in detail about the use of VMware's Site Recovery Manager as it provides the best mechanism. Before doing that, though, the following sections talk briefly about the other options.

Manual Disaster Recovery

When looking at implementing a manual data recovery plan, you need to ensure you are doing a few things that Site Recovery Manager would be automatically handling or assisting with. Many times, the use of manual methods is the result of a lack of sponsorship of the initiative in terms of funding; however, that does not mean the process cannot work. If you are creating a manual data recovery plan consider the following.

- Ensure data is being replicated/copied and is current with your RPO.

- Ensure your processes for restoration meet your RTO.

- Ensure the Disaster Recovery (DR) site hardware is supported and will support the load in the event of a disaster.

- Ensure the recovery processes work by performing regular DR tests.

- Ensure the runbook is updated regularly as network, application, and other requirements change.

By keeping these points in mind, your disaster recovery efforts will be successful; however, you will have to perform many of the steps manually.

Whereas storage replication was previously a condition for using Site Recovery Manager, the latest version now supports host-based replication. If you were previously unable to use Site Recovery Manager because of the storage replication requirement, you should reevaluate the product with host-based replication.

Site Recovery Manager

VMware offers a product called Site Recovery Manager that helps automate most of the process of recovering virtual machines during a disaster. The product allows for isolated testing to ensure recovery is possible in the event of an actual disaster as well as the ability to failback in version 5.0.

When installed at both the production and disaster recovery locations, the product provides for a centralized approach to defining replication and recovery plans. In prior versions, SRM relied on the storage itself to perform the replications and integrated with the storage using a supported Storage Replication Adapter (SRA). This limited the product for some entities with supported storage. Even those with supported storage devices in both locations might not have had matching storage solutions and, hence, no supported replication infrastructure in place.

SRM 5.0, however, has expanded its market base with the introduction of vSphere Replication (VR). This allows replication from one location to another, regardless of the type of storage on both ends. One or both ends can even be local or directly attached storage. SRM is also protocol independent so you can replicate among Fibre Channel, iSCSI, or NFS storage.

For more information on Site Recovery Manager, check out *Administering VMware Site Recovery Manager 5.0* by Mike Laverick. This book provides an in-depth discussion of the product, using it in a number of scenarios, and is a great read when defining a disaster recovery solution in a virtualized environment.

Physical to Virtual Conversions

When a virtualization infrastructure is implemented, the first virtual machine installed is typically going to be brand-new installations of Windows for your vCenter and SQL servers. Many times, a project like this also serves as a good time to clean up and move toward the latest server operating systems. Regardless at some point, you need to begin moving some of the existing physical workloads over and retaining their configurations.

VMware provides a free download for a product that will assist in this migration. VMware vCenter Converter Standalone 5.0 allows the conversion of physical systems as well as systems that are already virtualized. When performing physical to virtual conversions, you should be aware of the following things.

For all systems, you should do the following:

- **Prior to conversion**
  - Perform a survey of the server and its applications.
  - Identify server and application owners for approval and verification testing upon completion.
  - Identify performance and configuration of CPU/memory/disk versus actual usage.
  - Identify destination for virtual machine (host placement and storage placement).

- Identify and record network configurations.

- Identify downtime and schedule for system(s).

- **During conversion**

  - Place virtual machine on host and storage per design.

  - Adjust configurations of CPU/memory/disk as appropriate.

- **After conversion**

  - Remove nonpresent devices.

  - Remove legacy software.

  - Install VMware Tools.

  - Reconfigure the network.

  - Perform basic testing.

  - Verify functionality with server and application owners.

  - Fully uncable and remove decommissioned physical servers.

Issues and Troubleshooting

Physical to virtual conversions can fail to start. Typically, we have found this is because of one of the following reasons:

- No Permissions Admin$

- Firewall exists between server to be converted and vCenter

- Incorrect DNS configurations

In some cases, administrators have removed the admin$ share on a server, which is required for the vCenter Converter agent installation when installing remotely. You can install the client locally or re-create the share to resolve these issues.

When a firewall exists, it can cause a failure if certain ports are not reachable. VMware Knowledge Base article 1010056 details the required ports to be allowed through the firewall (see Appendix A for a link).

If DNS configurations are not correct on a source virtual machine, this can also cause failures. Ensure DNS is correct or update DNS so that the system to be converted can reach the vCenter server.

Besides these basic considerations, you should also consider a few special cases:

- Domain controllers

- Windows Server with OEM installations

- SQL, Exchange, and other applications servers

- Linux

- Virtual to virtual conversions (V2V)

Domain Controllers

Active Directory domain controllers have special considerations to take when looking at physical to virtual conversions. Although there are methods to perform a P2V conversion, it is our recommendation you don't and instead create new virtual servers. Domain controllers are extremely sensitive to hardware changes and a failure in following the P2V process at any step can cause major replication issues that will be visible throughout your infrastructure. Creating new servers allows for a clean and safer migration. The recommended process is as follows. Note this may vary depending on how many Active Directory domain controllers you have, their location, and whether they remain physical or not.

- Create one or more brand-new Windows virtual machines.

- Promote these two domain controllers using dcpromo.

- Ensure replication via the command line using the repadmin tool.

- Transfer FSMO roles.

- Transfer DHCP servers.

- Verify role transfer.

- If the domain controller is also a DNS server, ensure DNS is running on new systems.

- Power down physical domain controller and verify functionality. If no issues exist, power back on and demote existing physical systems using dcpromo (FSMO role will be transferred there also).

- Decommission physical hosts.

- Reconfigure DNS settings for servers/workstations to reflect any new IP addresses.

Windows Server with OEM Installations

Another case for consideration is any physical Windows servers that were originally installed with OEM media. Per Microsoft's licensing agreement, these licenses are tied to the original physical hardware and as a result the right to continue using the installed operating system does not carry over. Microsoft licensing is outside the scope of this book; however, two things can be drawn from this situation:

1. You are not in compliance with your licensing. You need to have or purchase an additional Microsoft server license.

2. You are running a version of Windows you are not licensed for. You need to either install a fresh instance of Windows using volume licensed media or perform an in-place upgrade using the volume licensed media.

If you have ignored these recommendations, you will find that once you bring the newly converted virtual machine online, it will require activation. With OEM installation, the key that is required to activate is not necessarily the one that was on the sticker on the box. With that said, you might be able to activate the software installation; however, you need to ensure you are in compliance with Microsoft licensing as soon as possible thereafter.

Although vendor background screens are typically a clear indication that OEM installations are present, you can also check the product ID for OEM to verify. If it is not present, you are fine. You can script this to check for multiple servers in your environments using various product and key software products that reveal this information. Additionally, you can use code like this PowerShell snippet to gather this information. The following code sets $Prod_ID to the ProductID of the machine it is run on:

```
$Prod_ID=(get-item 'HKLM:\Software\Microsoft\Windows NT\
  CurrentVersion').getvalue('ProductID')
```

SQL, Exchange, and Other Applications Servers

Although vCenter Converter will make multiple passes through your data, it is important to consider what could be lost in the transition time in between bringing the physical host down and the last time the data was copied. As a result, it is recommended that you stop all application services.

In addition, consider file shares. You may declare in an email that the server will be down this Saturday, but that doesn't stop someone from changing data. This data could end up being changed at a time of transition and would in effect be lost. Therefore, it is recommended that you unshare any file shares during the conversion process. Additionally, you should remove any temporary files or any data that is no longer needed. This greatly decreases the time involved when converting and optimizes the amount of physical storage being used.

Linux

This chapter has talked a lot about virtualizing Windows servers, but now the focus shifts to Linux servers. Linux servers follow a slightly different process and, as a result, there are some things you should be aware of. For starters, the process for Linux does not deploy an agent, but instead a helper virtual machine is deployed on the destination vSphere host. This helper machine will ultimately become the production virtual machine once it has copied all of the data from the physical Linux machine.

You should consider a few important things:

- You must ensure you have SSH access to the Linux machine when doing an online conversion and you must have root access when doing so.

- Only certain flavors of Linux are supported for online conversions. Presently, these are certain versions of Red Hat, SUSE, and Ubuntu.

- Customization during the conversion process is not supported for Linux guest operating systems.

V2V and Other Methods

Physical machines are not the only machines that may need to be brought into a new infrastructure. For example, you may have existing virtual machines running on storage not accessible to the new environment. You may also have these virtual machines running in a Hyper-V environment. Additionally, you may choose to do an offline conversion by using an imaging product. Regardless of the source, vCenter Converter allows for all of these options when using any of the following supported methods.

The following virtual machine formats are supported for cold conversion:

- Microsoft Hyper-V
- Microsoft Virtual Server
- Microsoft Virtual PC
- Parallels Desktop
- VMware Workstation, GSX Server, Player, Server, Fusion, ESX

The following image formats are supported:

- Symantec Backup Exec System Recovery
- Norton Ghost
- Acronis
- StorageCraft

Additionally, during the conversion process, you can convert any running Windows virtual machine by specifying a powered-on machine as the source.

Offline Boot Disc

When an offline conversion is desired in addition to the mentioned image formats, you can use the VMware vCenter Converter Boot CD. The boot CD is no longer provided as of vCenter Converter 4.3; however, it is still available for download with valid support for a vSphere 4.x Enterprise Edition or greater license. At the time of this writing, there are no current plans to release a vCenter Converter Boot CD for vSphere 5.0; however, version 4.0.1 build 16134 is the latest version and is supported for conversions from a source to a vCenter 5 infrastructure.

The offline boot disc is based on Windows PE and allows the import of network drivers to build a new image if required. The lack of network drivers is the most common reason the offline boot disc does not work.

Maintenance

Maintaining a vSphere-based virtual infrastructure is very important. After all, you have a large number of operating systems now running collectively on a much lesser amount of physical hardware in most cases. A failure to update for and then be exposed to a potential flaw may now put your entire infrastructure at risk instead of only some servers.

Why do organizations not properly maintain their vSphere environments? Everyone agrees with the criticality of maintaining servers whether it is through patches or regular release updates, but still it remains a large problem in many environments. In large part, the main driving force to perform any update is a result of an enhancement release that has added additional features.

Update Manager

One reason many administrators do not update their infrastructures is due to a lack of understanding of the process. Maybe they are new to VMware and never bothered to even install Update Manager with vCenter. Update Manager is not a requirement to patch systems but the process does become much more involved when using the command-line interface to do so. An administrator must download the update bundle and transfer it to each of the hosts. Then a command-line process must be invoked from each of the hosts. In the days before Update Manager, it is no wonder why some administrators might have chosen to patch less frequently or not at all.

vSphere is a hardened hypervisor and, as a result, needs much less patching and updating for vulnerabilities than a typical operating system. Many administrators, though, take this as a reason not to patch at all.

Some also entirely understand the advantages of Update Manager and have it installed and running. They realize how the effect of an issue with their vSphere infrastructures could now affect all their operating systems instead of just a handful. As a result, they view this increased impact of any updates as possibly negative. This may be the proper viewpoint as certain vulnerabilities may not be a high risk for their environments. They are further justified in their decision in knowing that the impact of any issues that occur in a virtual infrastructure can be huge if not properly planned. Perhaps the feature that is affected is also not something they are using. Being cautious and properly planning and testing for updates is certainly the way to go. To date, I have never worked directly with anyone who has been exploited by a VMware vulnerability. This is a true testament to the ability to harden the hypervisor and keep ahead of the curve with security exploits.

Again, that does not justify not patching. With the ever-increasing deployments of vSphere, it seems pretty reasonable to think the focus will continue to shift toward attacking these consolidated infrastructures powered by VMware. After all, wouldn't it be easier to bring down 10 vSphere hosts running 200 servers than to try to bring them down individually?

Update Manager is a patch-management solution provided by VMware with all versions of vCenter Server. It helps to automate the deployment of patches and updates and provides a means to maintain compliancy among your entire infrastructure. Its capabilities are not just limited to vSphere ESXi hosts either, as you can now patch many virtual appliances as well as extensions such as the Cisco Nexus 1000V and EMC PowerPath.

Formerly, Update Manager was capable of remediating Windows guest virtual machines by providing operating system and application patches. As of vSphere 5, however, this capability is no longer included. Interestingly, they licensed the technology from Shavlik, which they recently acquired. VMware now offers several other products that offer comparable capabilities. vCenter Protect Essentials and VMware Go both offer abilities to patch and manage guest operating systems. vCenter Protect Essentials provides for an on-premise solution that will patch and manage virtual machines. In the case of VMware Go, it is a cloud-based solution that also offers capabilities for help desk end-user portals. Both products also provide asset and configuration management capabilities that are geared toward the small to medium business market.

A major selling point of utilizing Update Manager to patch your vSphere servers is that when set up and used properly, it requires zero downtime to any of your virtual machines. There is no need to worry about having to have downtime twice for virtual machines for both the vSphere and guest patching. Utilizing DRS in conjunction with Maintenance mode, an administrator can deploy patches to a host with zero downtime to any of the virtual machines in the entire infrastructure.

Update Manager also allows the scheduling of updates. Simply create or attach a baseline to a set of hosts and choose a date and time to run the updates. These baselines can be assigned at the vCenter level or at the datacenter, cluster, or host level. Another useful ability of Update Manager is to stage and schedule virtual machine hardware and tools upgrades.

Patching Hosts Using Update Manager

With a DRS-enabled cluster and the use of Maintenance mode, patching hosts using Update Manager is a straightforward process; however, the following key areas are often overlooked:

- **Sizing the patch repository**—The patch repository can become quite large depending on the versions of vSphere you choose to implement over time. As a result, it is best practice to configure a shared repository outside of the vCenter server or server where Update Manager is installed when separated. VMware offers the vSphere Update Manager Sizing Estimator for download, which will aid in sizing not only the shared repository, but also the database itself.

- **Notification of new patches**—You will have a hard time knowing when to install updates if you do not know when they come out. The easiest way to be notified of new patches is by configuring email notifications under the Download Schedule of Update Manager.

- **Failure to consider compatibility and support**—There is a lot to consider when choosing to install updates. If you are running a solution where the vendor will only support virtual machines on a certain revision of the software, then you should clarify how these support policies are affected by updates. This is a rarity these days as solutions such as Cisco's unified communications on top of UCS software are fully supported by all updates at the time of release.

- **Failure to disable HA during an update**—If you have a smaller cluster of hosts, you might run into a failure if you do not disable HA during a host update. By default, this is not set but can be if you are going to run into this issue. Without doing so, if your cluster cannot support HA and you attempt a remediation, it will fail.

- **Failure to properly configure DNS**—If DNS is not properly configured, you will spend a lot of time troubleshooting why Update Manager is not working. It is highly dependent on DNS to be configured properly on both the vCenter and vSphere hosts. Failing to do so causes Update Manager to fail during the remediation.

Upgrading Hosts

VMware periodically releases new versions of vSphere that require an upgrade to vSphere. If an environment is healthy and no issues exist, we recommend using Upgrade Manager to upgrade the hosts in place. If, however, there are issues with your environment, consider wiping away each host and starting fresh.

You should also consider downtime in your environment for the upgrade. If your virtual machines are on shared storage backed by hosts that can vMotion among one another, you will be able to have much less downtime than an environment with virtual machines on local storage, for example. Different circumstances warrant different paths, so let's talk about some of the key items to consider when planning your upgrade.

Planning for vSphere Upgrades

Planning for vSphere upgrades requires investigating your environment from top to bottom to ensure you are presently free of any issues and have the appropriate pieces to perform a successful upgrade of your environment. In fact, before an upgrade is the perfect time for a health check to be performed by a VMware authorized partner. Although this section describes the important steps to consider, you might also want to take a look at the *vSphere Upgrade Guide* provided by VMware.

Upgrade Entitlement

Before you get too far along, you need to ensure you are eligible to upgrade. Upgrades are not at an additional cost when you have a valid support contract with VMware for your purchased licenses. If you have an eligible support contract, you can find both the software and licenses available in your VMware software and licensing portals. If you don't have an eligible support contract, you need to either renew your support or purchase additional licenses. In addition to support for vSphere, this is also a good time to ensure your hardware is still supported by your vendor before proceeding with an upgrade.

Feature Changes

Another consideration is changes that might have occurred between the old and new versions of vSphere. An example of this is an organization using Update Manager as part of vSphere 4 to patch its Windows guest. This functionality is no longer included as of vSphere 5; however, it can be acquired as part of vCenter Protect Essentials or Essentials Plus.

Hardware Compatibility

If your hardware is older, there is a chance that the hosts, storage, or IO devices might not be supported with the new release. Regardless of how new your equipment is, you should reference the *VMware Compatibility Guide* online to ensure the hardware will be supported after an upgrade. Although some people might not be concerned with hardware being fully supported, they should be advised that if it is not supported, there is a chance it will not work in some fashion. Be sure to check compatibility for your specific host. You will find that there may be several versions and revisions for popular brand models. Additionally, be sure to check your I/O devices and storage as well.

Database Compatibility

You need to be sure your database is supported with the new version of vCenter to which you will be upgrading. Many versions of SQL 2000 and 2005 are no longer supported despite their use, and you should consider upgrading the database servers if yours are not supported. Check out the VMware Product Interoperability Matrix online to verify your database software support before proceeding with any vCenter upgrades.

vCenter Support

You also need to ensure your vCenter server will support any older versions for hosts that are going to run for any period of time on an older version as part of that vCenter server. You can again check the VMware Product Interoperability Matrix online to verify this information. Pay close attention to the matrix, as shown in Figure 3.4. At the time of this writing, there is a known issue with VMware 4.0 U2 that does not allow it to be managed by a VMware vCenter server. This is a good example where a lot of people continue to make assumptions of the support to find out later that it does not work correctly.

Platform	VMware vCenter Server 5.0	VMware vCenter Server 4.1 U2	VMware vCenter Server 4.1 U1	VMware vCenter Server 4.1	VMware vCenter Server 4.0 U4	VMware vCenter Server 4.0 U3	VMware vCenter Server 4.0 U2	VMware vCenter Server 4.0 U1	VMware vCenter Server 4.0	VMware vCenter Server 2.5 U6
VMware ESXi 5.0	✓									
VMware ESX/ESXi 4.1 U2	✓	✓	✓	✓						
VMware ESX/ESXi 4.1 U1	✓	✓	✓	✓						
VMware ESX/ESXi 4.1		✓	✓	✓						
VMware ESX/ESXi 4.0 U4	✓	✓	✓	✓	✓	✓	✓	✓	✓	
VMware ESX/ESXi 4.0 U3	✓	✓	✓	✓	✓	✓	✓	✓	✓	
VMware ESX/ESXi 4.0 U2		✓	✓	✓	✓	✓	✓	✓	✓	
VMware ESX/ESXi 4.0 U1	✓	✓	✓	✓	✓	✓	✓	✓	✓	
VMware ESX/ESXi 4.0	✓	✓	✓	✓	✓	✓	✓	✓	✓	
VMware ESX/ESXi 3.5 U5	✓	✓	✓	✓	✓	✓	✓	✓	✓	✓
VMware ESX/ESXi 3.0.3 U1		✓	✓	✓	✓	✓				✓

Figure 3.4   vCenter Compatibility and Support Matrix

Additionally, you need to make sure vCenter is installed on a 64-bit operating system. If your existing vCenter server is older, you might not be able to directly upgrade anyway; however, if it is installed on a 32-bit operating system, you definitely need to install a fresh operating system.

In addition to support, you must also see if an upgrade is possible. As shown in Figure 3.5, you can see that, in general, there is direct upgrade available from 4.0 U1 up to vCenter 5.0 with the exception of 4.0 U4. Both 4.0 and 4.0 U4, and even 2.4 U6, however, can be upgraded to 4.1 U2. Once at 4.1 U2, they can be updated to vCenter 5.0 directly. Always check the VMware Product Interoperability Matrixes and *vSphere Upgrade Guide* for the most up-to-date support information. Again, remember there is a 64-bit requirement, so if you don't have a 64-bit server, you need to install a new version of Windows to support your new vCenter Server installation.

Platform	VMware vCenter Server 5.0	VMware vCenter Server 4.1 U2	VMware vCenter Server 4.1 U1	VMware vCenter Server 4.1	VMware vCenter Server 4.0 U4	VMware vCenter Server 4.0 U3	VMware vCenter Server 4.0 U2	VMware vCenter Server 4.0 U1	VMware vCenter Server 4.0	VMware vCenter Server 2.5 U6
VMware ESXi 5.0	✓									
VMware ESX/ESXi 4.1 U2	✓	✓	✓	✓						
VMware ESX/ESXi 4.1 U1	✓	✓	✓	✓						
VMware ESX/ESXi 4.1		✓	✓	✓						
VMware ESX/ESXi 4.0 U4	✓	✓	✓	✓	✓	✓	✓	✓	✓	
VMware ESX/ESXi 4.0 U3	✓	✓	✓	✓	✓	✓	✓	✓	✓	
VMware ESX/ESXi 4.0 U2		✓	✓	✓	✓	✓	✓	✓	✓	
VMware ESX/ESXi 4.0 U1	✓	✓	✓	✓	✓	✓	✓	✓	✓	
VMware ESX/ESXi 4.0	✓	✓	✓	✓	✓	✓	✓	✓	✓	
VMware ESX/ESXi 3.5 U5	✓	✓	✓	✓	✓	✓	✓	✓	✓	✓
VMware ESX/ESXi 3.0.3 U1		✓	✓	✓	✓	✓				✓

Figure 3.5   vCenter Upgrade Compatibility and Support Matrix

Dependencies

Outside of the core functionality in the vCenter server and the vSphere hosts, there exist some other pieces that need consideration as well. These are just some examples and you need to also consider any additional software or plug-ins that are used in your environment. Make sure to consider these pieces by verifying support by the vendor or within the *vSphere Upgrade Guide*:

- vCenter Update Manager
- vCenter License Server
- VMware View
- VMware Data Recovery
- Site Recovery Manager
- Third-party plug-ins like PowerPath

- Use of Nexus 1000V

- Any PowerShell or other scripting used for troubleshooting and reporting

Upgrade Paths

vSphere 5 is the first version of vSphere that has been released in only the ESXi flavor, so there is only one destination when upgrading to vSphere 5. You must also consider the source of the server and whether you have the option to upgrade.

The following is true about upgrading older versions of ESX and ESXi to vSphere 5.0. Note there are conditions where these items might not apply, so be sure to check the VMware Product Interoperability Matrixes and *vSphere Upgrade Guide* for the most up-to-date support information.

ESX & ESXi 3.5

- No direct upgrade available

- Upgrade to 4.x first

- Note that the partition layout might be incompatible with vSphere 5, so this can prohibit such an upgrade to 5.0

ESX & ESXi 4.0

- Direct upgrade available with Update Manager, interactively, or scripted

- Might not be compatible with all environments

- For example, ESX 4 hosts on SAN/SSD might not have optimal partitions and disks with multiple VMFS partitions cannot be upgraded

- Additionally, note that a host with any third-party vSphere Installation Bundles (VIB) may require using the ESXi Image Builder CLI to create a customized ESXi install ISO

And one last note on upgrading hosts. As of vSphere 5, the advanced version no longer exists and any customers with active support agreements for vSphere 4 Advanced are entitled to vSphere Enterprise.

Order of Operations

When laying out your plan for an upgrade, you must consider the order in which you are going to do so. Outside of the vCenter and vSphere hosts themselves, you need to make sure you upgrade to supported code and firmware for your storage and other devices ahead of time. Additionally, be sure you have proper backups of the necessary components. For vCenter, you need at minimum a backup copy of the database as well as Secure Socket Layer (SSL) certificates from the server. For the hosts themselves, you need to have good documentation on their configuration as well as a backup copy of all virtual machines. This holds especially true if you are upgrading a host with virtual machines running on local storage. For virtual machines on shared storage, you need to ensure backups exist as you will be upgrading our virtual hardware and VMware Tools later on.

In general, follow these steps to perform an upgrade:

1. Run the vCenter Host Agent Pre-Upgrade Checker. This can be found on the vCenter installation media and is a great verification tool to ensure the likelihood of a successful upgrade.

2. Upgrade or install a new vCenter server.

3. Upgrade or install a new Update Manager.

4. Upgrade or install other plug-ins and third-party packages.

5. Upgrade or install vSphere on hosts.

6. Upgrade VMFS.

7. Upgrade virtual machine tools and hardware.

Methods for Upgrading vSphere

As discussed previously, to perform your vCenter upgrade, you can either upgrade the software in place if supported or install a fresh vCenter server. You can then choose to either start completely fresh, redefine roles and other vCenter configurations, or import the database and continue from there.

For vSphere hosts, you not only have the option of upgrading or starting fresh, but you also have several methods to perform the upgrade. When possible, we recommend building new hosts and bringing configurations over.

In previous versions of vSphere, the Host Update Utility was included on the vCenter installation media for performing host upgrades on a host-by-host basis. Note that this is no longer the case and you must upgrade your hosts by either using vSphere 5 media or through Update Manager.

Manual Upgrade

You may manually perform an upgrade to a host using the ESXi installation media by performing an interactive or scripted upgrade. It is recommended you disconnect all storage from the host as this greatly reduces the amount of time required for the upgrade.

When upgrading a host, you have three options:

- Upgrade ESXi, Preserve VMFS Datastore or Force Migrate ESXi, Preserve VMFS Datastore

- Install ESXi, Preserve VMFS Datastore

- Install ESXi, Overwrite VMFS Datastore

The first option will vary if any custom VIBs are not included with the vSphere 5 media. If that is the case, Force Migrate ESXi replaces Upgrade ESXi. Make sure to back up any items on the local VMFS datastore beforehand and especially when choosing to overwrite the VMFS datastore.

In addition to performing an interactive upgrade, you may also choose to perform a scripted installation. For full details on creating a scripted installation, including adding custom drivers and third-party VIBs, check out the *vSphere Upgrade Guide*.

Update Manager

When using Update Manager to upgrade hosts, an orchestrated host upgrade can occur that allows not only for vSphere host installation, but the installation of VMware Tools and the upgrade of virtual hardware.

Update Manager does have some limitations that you may encounter. Recall from the earlier discussion of upgrade paths that there are some limitations even when following a supported path. Update Manager cannot be used to upgrade an ESX 4.x host if it was previously upgraded from 3.x as a result of insufficient space in the /boot partition. This problem is not unique as it is possible an ESX 4.x host may also not have the proper amount of space.

If you are not installing a fresh version of vSphere, it is recommended to use Update Manager because it greatly eases the upgrade process. The use of Update Manager does a better job of preventing erroneous actions and disallows things such as upgrading the virtual machine hardware before installing VMware Tools.

Host Upgrades   Upgrading a host requires the creation of a host upgrade baseline. Additionally, you are required to import the ESXi image to be used for upgrades.

You may choose to have separate baselines and separate images in the repository. For example, you may have different images based on hardware for the hosts, which may be of different vendor types and contain different third-party VIBs.

You cannot roll back to the previous version of ESX/ESXi when upgrading with Update Manager, so, as always, make sure you have the configuration of your host documented and the proper backups of all virtual machines in place before proceeding with any upgrades.

Virtual Machine Upgrades   Upgrading virtual machines after an upgrade requires using an existing baseline or the creation of a baseline group. You cannot upgrade VM hardware until the virtual machine is running the latest version of VMware Tools. Update Manager makes sure this happens to avoid these operations not occurring in sequence.

By default, the following two baselines are created:

- VMware Tools Upgrade to Match Host
- VM Hardware Upgrade to Match Host

When scheduling the update, you can granularly schedule separate virtual machines depending on the following power states. For example, you might want to schedule any powered-on machine later because they will require downtime, as shown in Figure 3.6. Your options for scheduling virtual machine updates include the following:

- Powered On
- Powered Off
- Suspended

An orchestrated upgrade of virtual machines is not required but greatly reduces the time it takes to remediate a large number of virtual machines at the same time. If you would rather manually remediate the virtual machines, simply upgrade VMware Tools on each virtual machine and then power off the virtual machine to perform the virtual hardware upgrade.

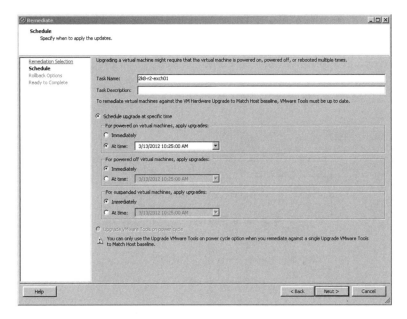

Figure 3.6   Scheduling Update Manager Updates

Monitoring

Like maintenance, monitoring is sometimes forgotten with a virtual infrastructure. Many organizations continue their monitoring of their guest virtual machines without a consideration for the hosts themselves. Others consider the hosts but don't have the proper monitoring software, licensing, or understanding of how or what to monitor in the virtual infrastructure. Regardless of the reason, the need to monitor the underlying components of a virtual infrastructure remains high.

Alerting

I once had a customer contact me who did not understand why he didn't receive an email notification that one of his storage paths had lost redundancy. He had logged in to his vCenter server and noticed the down host, which had been offline for two days. Although this showed off how well the cluster handled the failure of the host, it was a major point of concern for him because he didn't know the host had failed. In this case, the customer had not fully configured the alarms in vCenter. This section discusses the process required to set up alarms as well as some common issues encountered.

For starters, you need to configure the mail setting in vCenter Server.

To do this, go to Administration, vCenter Server Settings from the vSphere Client. Next, configure the SMTP server and appropriate sender account, as shown in Figure 3.7.

Figure 3.7   Configuring vCenter Email Settings

You need to configure both an SMTP and a sending account. Additionally, you need to ensure your SMTP server can accept relayed messages from your vCenter server.

This is a step that nearly everyone configures during the default install. A common problem, though, is this is where many people stop. By default, vCenter 5 has 54 alarms defined; however, to set up any type of SNMP or email alerting, actions must be individually defined for each alarm.

Defining Actions for Alarms

For most alarms, only three actions can be defined. You may define an action once or multiple times for each alarm, and you may define multiple types of actions for a single alarm. The actions that are available to be configured are as follows.

- Send a Notification Email
- Send a Notification Trap
- Run a Command

Two monitor types, however, have the capability of performing specific actions. The Alarm Type Monitor for Virtual Machines may take the following actions in addition to sending an email, sending an SNMP trap, or running a command:

- Enter Maintenance Mode
- Exit Maintenance Mode
- Enter Standby
- Exit Standby
- Reboot Host
- Shutdown Host

The Alarm Type Monitor for Hosts may take the following actions in addition to the three actions mentioned—sending an email, sending an SNMP trap, or running a command:

- Power On VM
- Power Off VM
- Suspend VM
- Reset VM
- Migrate VM
- Reboot Guest On VM
- Shutdown Guest On VM

For the following Alarm Type Monitors, the only three actions are to send a notification email, send a notification trap, or run a command:

- Clusters
- Datacenters
- Datastores
- vSphere Distributed Switches
- Distributed Port Groups

- Datastore Clusters
- vCenter Server

The process for defining actions for alarms is pretty straightforward; however, there are a few things to be aware of.

First, as mentioned, 54 alarms are defined by default. Defining all 54 alarms individually would take a long time and would likely result in a few of them being configured incorrectly due to an occasional keystroke error. Don't worry, though, because PowerShell can be used to automate the creation of these actions and is discussed shortly.

Second, when you are defining actions, you must define when the action will occur and how often notification will occur for issues that persist. By default, you receive an email notification only when going from a yellow to a red state. There are four configurable options to consider:

- Green→Yellow
- Yellow→Red
- Red→Yellow
- Yellow→Green

Let's stop for a moment to talk about which of these four you will want to be notified of. If you are relying on SNMP traps being sent to your existing monitoring software, you may choose to have very little to no email notifications. Many smaller environments do not rely on SNMP notifications or still may require email notifications outside of their existing monitoring solutions. For environments with no other monitoring, it is best to configure all of the default alarms and some additional ones as well. These additional recommendations as well as automating the process are discussed in just a bit.

So you now have defined actions for all of your desired alarms as well as the severity changes you would like to be notified of and the amount of times you would like to be notified if the issue persists. That brings us to another common thing to consider for a new implementation.

We have witnessed some environments that simply forgot to allow the vCenter server to use the mail server as a relay. After all, the vCenter server may be a new addition to an environment and would not have been previously configured to relay email messages from the SMTP server. If you are unsure if the mail server is allowing relay for the host and do not have access to the email server to check, you may try the following:

```
telnet mailservername.vmware.com 25
helo vmware.com
```

There is still one more thing to be aware of. Even after all of this, you might find you are not being notified of some issues, for example when storage path redundancy is lost. This is because some triggers are left unset by default, as shown in Figure 3.8. When set to Unset, alarms do not show in vCenter; however, they are sent to email or as SNMP traps if configured. As you can see for the case of lost storage path redundancy, the status for each event is not set.

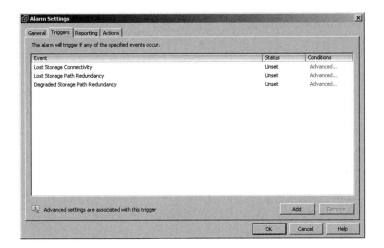

Figure 3.8   Unset vCenter Alarms

The following is a list of the other default alarms that are not set up:

- Unmanaged workload detected on Storage I/O Control (SIOC)-enabled datastore (this is disabled by default)

- VMkernel NIC not configured correctly

- Network uplink redundancy degraded

- Health Status Changed Alarm

- License Error

- Exit Standby Error

- Migration Error

- Host Connection Failure

- Virtual Machine Error

- Host Error

- No Compatible Host for Secondary VM
- Timed Out Starting Secondary VM

Two of the default alarms also are not configurable. These alarms are triggered via the vSphere API and can only be modified as such:

- Datastore Capability Alarm
- Thin-Provisioned LUN Capacity Exceeded

When creating actions, you just need to select an SNMP action in addition to or instead of an email notification so that a trap is sent. You may also enable SNMP traps for each individual host if desired. This may be beneficial in the event of a vCenter server outage as the individual hosts themselves will not communicate any status back otherwise.

Considerations for Tweaking Default Alarms

Some of the default alarms may have some notification options that are less than desirable for your environment. For example, you may have an environment that is strictly testing for internal IT staff. You may decide you still want all the alarms but fully accept that the vSphere hosts in question will likely be pegged pretty hard in terms of memory at certain times of the day. After all, this may be older hardware with lesser memory. You still, however, want to know if there is a consistent condition where memory is steady at 95% or greater for 30 minutes or more.

In this case, by default, the Host Memory Usage alarm warning triggers a warning when host memory usage is above 90% for 5 minutes. Also by default, an alert triggers when host memory usage is above 95% for 5 minutes. By setting both values to 5% higher and to lengths of 30 minutes, you do not get repeated alerts for expected high memory conditions, but do get notified when the issue becomes persistent enough where it may warrant finding additional memory for these hosts.

In closing, you can see that there is a lot to consider even when looking specifically at just vCenter alarms. Walking away from this discussion on alarms, remember the following key points:

- Consider that the alarms can be defined at many levels. Depending on your infrastructure, you might want to define alarms at the vCenter, datacenter, cluster, or individual host level. For that matter, you may also want to get even more granular and enable alarms on specific virtual machines, datastores, datastore clusters, and virtual distributed switches.

- Consider that triggers may have multiple actions that trigger based on both actions happening or one or the other.

- Consider how often you want to be notified and of what state changes you would like to be notified. Too many alerts can become just as big of a problem as not enough alerts at times if you begin tuning them out.

Before moving on to the next section, some assistance in setting up these alarms using PowerShell was promised. With just a few modifications, the provided PowerShell script allows you to easily set up all or as many of the default alarms as you would like. Note that you need to configure the alarms mentioned that are not configured by default to your liking for your environment. Although this still leaves some manual configuration, you no longer have to enter an email address for any of the alarms. It is our recommendation that you start by configuring all vCenter alarms and remove alarms that are not necessary for your environment.

You can download this script from http://www.seancrookston.com/set_alarms.ps1 (see Appendix A for a link).

Verifying Configurations

Another important component of operating a vSphere infrastructure is configuration management. When talking about configuration management, the concern is with ensuring configurations are not unknowingly changed or drift from their intended configurations. You want configurations to match their intended configuration and be consistent across the environment. For example, you want your hosts to be running on a certain build of vSphere and to be consistent with the other hosts within the same cluster.

vCenter Operations Enterprise versions include vCenter Configuration Manager, which provides the ability to monitor configuration virtual infrastructure configurations. vCenter Operations are discussed in further detail in Chapter 4, "Managing the Environment."

Even with a product like vCenter Operations, you still need to implement the most important part of a solid configuration management strategy. Policies and procedures for documenting configuration are the foundation to maintaining an environment with consistent and desired configurations.

When thinking about the configurations, the goal is to maintain many items that might not seem obvious initially. The following is a list of some of the pieces in your virtual infrastructure that might have configurations—in terms of software or firmware—to track and ensure are desired and consistent. Keep in mind this list is brief and we could easily drill even deeper.

- vCenter Server configuration

    - Cluster configuration

    - High Availability configuration

    - DRS configuration

    - Update Manager configuration

- vSphere host configuration

    - vSphere drivers and operating software

    - HBA drivers and firmware

    - NIC drivers and firmware

- IP network configuration

- Storage network configuration

- Storage firmware and software versions

- Virtual guest configuration

Host Profiles

If a product like Operations Manager is not a fit, you may also use Host Profiles. This feature is included with the Enterprise Plus level of vCenter licensing and is of great assistance with managing the delivery of consistent configurations. Additionally, you may use Scheduled Tasks in vCenter to define a scheduled compliance check that will notify you daily of any configuration drift.

After you've configured your first host to the desired gold state, you can simply create a profile using this host as a reference host. Then you can take your baseline profile and apply it to other hosts or clusters. You will be prompted to enter dynamic information, such as network information during the application, but other configuration settings will be applied consistently to your hosts.

At any time, you can check the host's compliance against the profile or receive notification via email when a drift in configuration occurs. When the time comes to make a change to your standard configuration, the process is just as easy. Simply update your reference host's configuration and then update the profile and reapply the configuration to your other hosts.

Even if you do not have Enterprise Plus licensing, you should consider using Host Profiles during your setup as part of your 60-day evaluation licensing.

Health Check

So far, this chapter has discussed ways to operationally maintain the environment through updates and alerts. Another important operational step is to perform regular health checks of your environment. This may consist of a physical inspection as well as checking configurations. You may also be ensuring your configured alarms are configured as expected and manually checking for issues just in case. You may also be looking for drifts in configuration based on your organization's standardized configuration.

These are all important things to do and there are many community resources that can assist in these efforts. One such resource is a daily health check script developed by Alan Renouf called vCheck, detailed further in Appendix A.

This script creates a daily report that gives a great report of the environment, including items such as snapshots and new virtual machines that have been created. The setup process has been made easy with an install script, and a great demo video is included on the site for guidance in setting the script up.

Continuing the discussion of performing health checks, another reason to do a health check might be to get a new perspective on the current state of the environment. You might think to yourself, "Well, nothing has changed in this environment in the last three months." Considering that perhaps nothing has changed in the environment, you also need to consider what has changed externally to your environment. This doesn't strictly refer to the storage or networking attached to your vSphere hosts, although checking on these is equally important. Technology is often updated or at times has vulnerabilities due to security flaws in the product.

Bugs, workarounds, patches, and best practices are regularly released and updated. Many individuals barely have the time to perform their regular day-to-day duties, and this information can be difficult to find at times. This is where the aid of someone focused on vSphere technologies is of great advantage.

VMware's Health Check Delivery

VMware offers a Health Check service that can greatly aid in this need. Any of the information that is used during this process is available to anyone and you could use scripts like the ones mentioned to verify much of the same information. The time to do so could be substantial and unless you have significant experience across many environments, there may be the risk that you are missing something. The health check delivery has many big advantages, such as the following:

- Consultants will add in their experiences recently as well as perform additional checks.

- Consultants will have at minimum a VCP.

- Quick collection of data for analysis will be performed by an expert.

The result of the engagement is a report and in-depth analysis of the environment with suggestions and remediation. The suggestions are based on best-practice configuration and known issues across a wide range of industries and environments.

Operating the Environment Summary

This chapter focused on the operating phase of a virtualization infrastructure. You learned about many tools and methods to operate and monitor on a daily basis in addition to best practices and methods for continuing to bring existing physical workloads into your virtual infrastructure.

This chapter also discussed methods for monitoring and alerting of issues in the virtual infrastructure. From an operational perspective, you have covered the grounds of day-to-day management of your virtual infrastructure.

Moving forward, you need to monitor your environment's performance and capacity for growth. This is discussed in the following chapter.

Chapter 4

Managing the Environment

Capacity Management

After the infrastructure is deployed, the work does not stop there. As automated as a vSphere virtual infrastructure is, it still must be managed on an ongoing basis because workloads fluctuate and business needs change. This chapter examines managing the infrastructure as it grows.

Storage Capacity Management

Storage is the only hardware component that impacts all of the hosts in a vSphere cluster because it is a shared resource. If storage capacity runs low on a datastore, it can affect virtual machines on all the hosts because they are housed on the shared storage. For this reason, storage capacity management is the most important capacity management function in the virtual infrastructure.

Planning for Growth

Managing the storage capacity that is available in the virtual infrastructure is much easier than it was in the early days of VMware. There are built-in tools available for vSphere infrastructures that help the administrator manage existing storage capacity much more efficiently. Some of the tools available include the following:

- **Datastore clusters and Storage DRS**—Storage DRS helps administrators by automatically choosing an appropriate datastore for newly provisioned virtual machines. It can also automatically balance the virtual machines across datastores in a single datastore cluster. The metrics that Storage DRS uses to make placement and balancing decisions include used capacity of a datastore.

- **Thin provisioning**—Thin provisioning is the ability to allocate only what is used on demand to a virtual disk (VMDK). For example, a virtual machine operating system may see a 50GB VMDK when it only takes up 20GB worth of space. The VMDK will start out at 20GB and grow to the configured 50GB. The idea behind thin provisioning is that a given workload will not use all of the space available to it. The actual provisioning of the storage can be more efficient because it will not likely use all of the storage available to it.

Keep the following things in mind when using thin provisioned VMDKs:

- Thin provisioned disks in Microsoft operating system VMs should not be formatted using the Full Format option because a Full Format writes zeros to the entire disk, causing the thin provisioned VMDK to inflate to its full size. The Quick Format option should be used instead to keep the disk thin provisioned.

- Thin provisioning also should be used with appropriate alarms to monitor datastore usage so that thin provisioned disks do not grow too large on an overprovisioned datastore. A simple task, such as defragmenting a thin provisioned virtual disk, can cause the disk to grow. As a result, it is not recommended to run defragmentation utilities. These alarms should include the thin provisioning–specific "Datastore disk overallocation (%)".

- Decide operationally what can be tolerated as far as overallocation of datastore resources and set the alarms to account for this.

Host Capacity Management

Although storage capacity management affects the entire virtual infrastructure, decisions made on host capacity in the beginning can have a significant strategic impact as well. This section discusses the considerations of a scale-out versus a scale-up architecture decision. This decision can affect items like management overhead, consolidation ratios, and software licensing.

Scale Out Versus Scale Up

The scale-out versus scale-up discussion has been going on for quite a while. It has recently heated up again with vSphere 5 vRAM entitlement licensing. The following section describes what is meant by scale out versus scale up.

Scale-Out and Scale-Up Architecture

A scale-out architecture in vSphere uses lower VM consolidation ratios across many smaller hosts. The idea here is that the virtual infrastructure can start small and scale out as more virtual machines are added to the infrastructure. A scale-up architecture is one that uses higher VM consolidation ratios across fewer larger hosts. The idea here is that the virtual infrastructure can stay consistent with fewer hosts to manage.

This section discusses some advantages and disadvantages of a scale-out architecture to gain a better understanding of the advantages and disadvantages of both scale-out and scale-up architecture. The advantages of one type of architecture tend to be disadvantages for the other, as shown in Table 4.1.

Table 4.1. Advantages and Disadvantages of a Scale-Out Architecture

Advantages	Disadvantages
Lower up-front costs	Higher software licensing costs
More choices for Distributed Resource Scheduler to base its load balancing decisions on	Lower chances of processor feature parity for vMotion as the infrastructure scales out
Spreading the risk out across more infrastructure assets	More management overhead versus a scale-up architecture

Let's take a more detailed look at these advantages and disadvantages:

- **Lower up-front costs**—There's no denying that the up-front costs for a scale-out architecture strategy are less. The reason a scale-out architecture can be appealing up front is that you can start small and "scale out" with lower-cost servers as the infrastructure grows. This tends to be a very tactical decision instead of a long-term strategic decision. Also, one of the most obvious advantages of server virtualization is hardware consolidation. A scale-out architecture can take the hardware consolidation advantage off the table. A scale-up architecture tends to lower the total cost of ownership of the infrastructure in the long term.

- **More choices for Distributed Resource Scheduler**—Distributed Resource Scheduler uses many inputs to determine cluster imbalance. There are constraints to consider (affinity, anti-affinity rules, etc.) and there are also resource inputs regarding CPU and memory. The scale-out versus scale-up decision mostly affects CPU load balancing. Memory capacity can easily be added to a host to scale up. CPU capacity is typically fixed in a host (two- or four-socket systems are the normal layout).

  By having more CPU sockets available across more hosts, there are more chances for the DRS algorithm to recommend load balancing moves across the cluster. This is only advantageous if your workloads are more CPU bound than memory bound. This determination goes back to capacity planning. In our experience, the majority of workloads that we have worked with have been more memory bound than CPU bound. If your workloads do happen to be CPU bound, then mark "DRS load balancing choices" as an advantage for a scale-out architecture.

- **Spreading the risk across more infrastructure assets**—Anytime server workloads are consolidated into fewer hardware assets, the risk is consolidated and concentrated into those few hardware assets. Let's simplify the concept of hardware failure risk into a single entity for a moment and divide it out among hardware assets. Clearly, in this simple model, the more hardware assets we have, the less risk is associated with each piece of hardware. However, this is not the most correct way to look at hardware failure risk.

  Look at it like the lottery. The more numbers you play on any given drawing, the higher chance there is that you'll win. It can be argued that, just as with the lottery, the more hardware you have, the higher probability that a piece of hardware will fail. In the case of hardware failure, you are not trying to "win the lottery." By scaling up instead of out, you may actually decrease your chances of suffering a hardware failure, especially if that hardware is as redundant as possible.

  So, why is spreading the risk across more infrastructure assets an advantage? It is an advantage because instead of decreasing your chances of a hardware failure, you are decreasing the affected workloads should a hardware failure occur. You are consolidating fewer workloads onto many servers.

  We often hear that scale out can be more cost effective from this standpoint because cheaper, less-redundant hardware can be purchased. The argument is that an individual host server failure does not matter because there are many more hosts to take on the workload. We would caution people not to immediately run with this line of thinking.

  From a pure workload perspective, this line of thinking is true. A scale-out architecture does offer more hosts and, therefore, could potentially offer more resources in the event of a failure. However, more than just pure workload must be considered. What if the application on a virtual machine does not tolerate hard failures that well? The risk of application failure or data loss must also be considered along with hardware failure. For this reason, it is not recommended to place production workloads on nonredundant or less-redundant host servers.

We've discussed some of the advantages of a scale-out architecture model. Let's take a look at some of the disadvantages:

- **Higher software licensing costs**—Many software vendors still use a licensing model that ties licenses to physical assets. If this is the case, the software licensing costs for a scale-out model increase. Obviously, a scale-out model requires more vSphere CPU licenses. However, let's look at how it can affect other licensing.

For example, let's look at Microsoft Operating System Environment (OSE) licensing. An Operating System Environment is the operating system license (e.g., Windows Server 2008). Microsoft happens to tie its OSE licenses to a physical asset instead of the virtual machine. To date, this is how the Microsoft OSE licensing works:

- A Microsoft OSE license is tied to the host server, not the VM.

- A Standard OSE license entitles the use of one OSE per host server.

- Two standard OSE licenses would allow two OSEs per server, and so on.

- An Enterprise OSE license entitles the use of four OSEs per host server.

- A Datacenter OSE license entitles the use of an infinite amount of OSEs per server.

- An OSE license cannot move from one physical server to another physical server except once every 90 days.

This licensing policy is problematic in a vSphere infrastructure that utilizes features like vMotion and specifically DRS. With DRS set to fully automated, workloads (OSEs) can move from host to host at any time. This may violate the "once every 90 days" movement constraint of the Microsoft licensing. The most effective way to license host servers to avoid licensing compliance issues is to use Datacenter licensing for each host in the vSphere cluster.

To further clarify this licensing decision, take a look at a simple Microsoft OSE licensing scenario:

- You have 100 Windows Server VMs that need to be licensed.

- You have 6 dual-socket CPU vSphere hosts in the same HA/DRS cluster that will support these VMs. This is a consolidation ratio of approximately 17 VMs per host.

- The DRS cluster setting is fully automatic.

- If you go with Standard OSE licensing, you need to purchase 600 licenses.

- If you go with Enterprise OSE licensing, you need to purchase 150 licenses.

- If you go with Datacenter OSE licensing, you need to purchase 12 licenses (Datacenter is licensed per CPU).

Clearly, in this scenario, the most scalable option is to use Windows Server Datacenter licensing. If you are using a scale-out model that has a consolidation ratio of 10 VMs per host, 10 physical host servers will be required. Instead of 12 Datacenter licenses, 20 Datacenter licenses will be required. This increases the OSE licensing costs along with the vSphere licensing costs. From a licensing perspective, a scale-up model is more cost effective in this scenario.

- **Lower chances of processor feature parity for vMotion as the infrastructure scales out**—vMotion will never work between a host with an AMD CPU and a host with an Intel processor.

For vMotion to work, the processors among the hosts in the cluster should ideally match.

There is a workaround for hosts that may have different CPUs from the same manufacturer to allow vMotion. This feature is called Enhanced vMotion Capability (EVC). Although EVC may allow vMotion to occur between different hosts, there may be some drawbacks. Let's examine how EVC works.

EVC works by masking CPU features to the lowest common CPU feature set within the vSphere cluster. When you enable EVC, you choose an EVC baseline that is equal to the lowest CPU family that you have in your cluster. For example, at the time of this writing, there are five generations of Intel CPU baselines and four generations of AMD CPU baselines to choose from:

Intel:

- Meron
- Penryn
- Nehalem
- Westmere
- Sandy Bridge

AMD:

- Opteron Generation 1
- Opteron Generation 2
- Opteron Generation 3
- Opteron Generation 3 (no 3DNow!)
- Opteron Generation 4

More information on the EVC Baselines and CPU compatibility can be found in VMware KB article 1003212 (see Appendix A, "Additional Resources").

For example, if your lowest family of Intel CPU was "Nehalem," you would set the EVC baseline for the cluster to "Nehalem." Now, if you add hosts with newer CPU generations to the cluster, you can still vMotion between the older hosts and the newer hosts because only the "Nehalem" CPU features are presented to the hosts and virtual machines.

This is great for backward compatibility. However, the EVC feature is masking CPU features that could otherwise be useful in the vSphere cluster. When utilizing a scale-up architecture, there are fewer hosts. So, it is easier to keep the hosts uniform in the cluster by refreshing the hosts at the same time. If a scale-out architecture is used, there are more hosts. So, a staggered refresh cycle is probably more feasible. The hosts in a scale-out architecture are likely different; therefore, EVC may need to be utilized for vMotion to occur. When deciding on a scale-out architecture, you may not be able to get the most out of your investment in hosts with newer CPUs.

- **More management overhead versus a scale-up architecture**—One disadvantage of a scale-out architecture is the management overhead that is associated with this particular architecture strategy. A scale-out architecture requires more hardware, more licensing, more patching, and so on. The more moving parts in the infrastructure, the more complex it will be. A complex infrastructure requires more decisions to be made. Management overhead can appear in the form of decisions that now must be made about the infrastructure that might not need to be made in scale-up infrastructure.

Let's think about virtualizing vCenter on the same cluster it manages for a moment. This is not an unusual scenario. However, a scale-out architecture may need additional considerations that are not needed in a scale-up architecture. For example, you might not think twice about letting DRS/HA move vCenter wherever it needs to in a three-host, scale-up architecture. However, you might consider restricting vCenter movement and recovery to just a few hosts in a ten-host, scale-out architecture. That way, in the event of an outage where vCenter needs to be restarted manually, you can easily find vCenter.

This is just one example of the management overhead involved in a scale-out architecture. It might not just be about more hardware to manage. Patching, hardware, and design considerations all play a part in the decision to choose a scale-out architecture. You must determine the considerations and weigh them when choosing a scale-out or scale-up architecture.

So, should you scale out or scale up? There are certainly advantages and disadvantages to both approaches. In the long term, we feel that a scale-up architecture is technically and financially superior to a scale-out architecture. We also realize that a scale-up architecture is not always feasible. We have given some advantages and disadvantages of a scale-out architecture to guide your decision.

One question we continue to receive is how vRAM entitlement affects the decision to scale out or scale up. The short answer is that it should not affect your decision. Let's review how vRAM entitlement works.

vRAM entitlement is a concept that came with vSphere 5. vRAM is defined as the amount of RAM that is assigned to any given virtual machine. A vRAM entitlement comes with each CPU license of vSphere 5 with the editions that are licensed per CPU instead of as a package. The vRAM entitlements at the time of this writing are as follows:

- vSphere Standard 1 CPU - 32GB vRAM

- vSphere Enterprise 1 CPU - 64GB vRAM

- vSphere Enterprise Plus 1 CPU - 96GB vRAM

- vSphere Essentials and Essentials Plus Kit - 192GB maximum pooled vRAM

The vRAM is pooled per vCenter instance. For example, if you had three dual-socket vSphere Enterprise Plus hosts in a single vCenter instance, you would have a total of 576GB of pooled vRAM. Some hosts may use more vRAM than others. In total, it would be uncommon to use all of the pooled vRAM available in this environment. However, what if you do need more vRAM? Well, you would simply purchase additional CPU licenses of vSphere 5.

The argument for scale out in relation to vRAM entitlement that we have heard is:

"If I need to purchase extra CPU licenses in order to increase my vRAM entitlement, why not just add more hosts to take advantage of those licenses?"

This is one of those situations where it is appropriate to state that just because you can do something, doesn't mean you should do something. If the extra CPU capacity is not needed, you should not add complexity and management overhead to the infrastructure just for the sake of using CPU licenses. There are valid reasons for a scale-out architecture, but vRAM entitlement is not one of them.

Networking Capacity Management

Networking is something that has long been taken for granted in a virtual infrastructure. If there was proper connectivity and redundancy, things simply worked. In some instances, that may still be the case today. However, as consolidation ratios grow and networks become more complex, there is a need for networking capacity management. This section discusses some strategies for managing the capacity of the virtual infrastructure network.

Planning for Growth

Capacity management for the networking components of a vSphere infrastructure is something that is often overlooked. The reality is that most workloads will not come close to saturating the bandwidth or other features of vSphere virtual networking. However, you should still be aware of the capabilities so that you can make solid design decisions when thinking about networking for the virtual infrastructure.

When thinking about scalable capacity for the infrastructure, it is important to first decide what general vSphere architecture will be used from a networking standpoint. Let's review those architectures in Figures 4.1, 4.2, and 4.3.

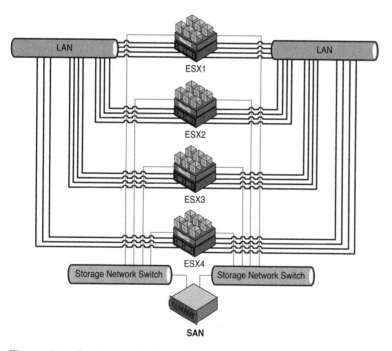

Figure 4.1 Traditional 1GbE Architecture

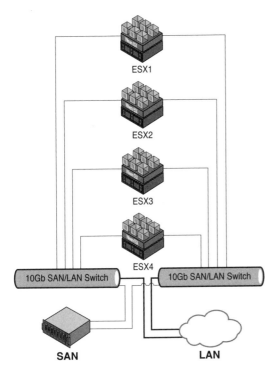

Figure 4.2   Converged Rackmount Architecture

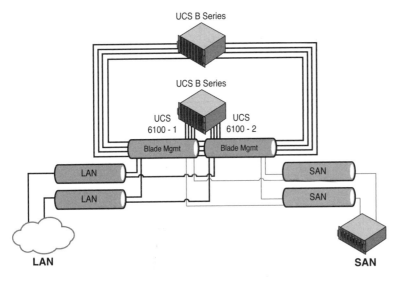

Figure 4.3   Converged Blade Architecture

Let's review how these different architectures scale from a networking standpoint:

- Traditional 1GbE architecture

  - This architecture scales linearly with the number of hosts.

  - The more hosts you add, the more upstream network ports you need.

  - It is not uncommon to have eight to ten NIC ports per vSphere host in this architecture.

  - For example, a four-host vSphere cluster may need 40 NIC ports, requiring two new 24-port switches for local area network (LAN) traffic alone.

- Converged rackmount architecture

  - This architecture scales linearly with the number of hosts.

  - The more hosts you add, the more upstream network ports you need.

  - Because the infrastructure is 10GbE, it is not uncommon to only have two to four 10GbE NIC ports per vSphere host in this architecture.

  - For example, a four-host vSphere cluster may need 16 NIC ports.

- Converged blade architecture

  - Scaling is based on actual bandwidth needs.

  - Adding more hosts does not necessarily mean that more upstream network ports need to be added.

  - Because the infrastructure is 10GbE and scaling is based on actual bandwidth needs, the port count is drastically reduced when compared with either the traditional 1GbE or converged rackmount architectures.

  - For example, if less than 10Gb is needed for bandwidth, you may only need 4 upstream switch ports connected for redundancy.

If you were to examine these three architectures for bandwidth and port count efficiency, the converged blade architecture would be the clear choice. However, in a blade architecture, the risk is consolidated so redundancy is even more important. For example, if a chassis is lost in a blade architecture, it could affect multiple hosts. Make sure there is a plan in place to recover from this. There are also other nontechnical factors to think about when designing a vSphere architecture. There is no one perfect architecture, and you must weigh the benefits of these architecture decisions against your own organizational budget and timeline.

The following list offers some general recommendations to help you make your decision:

- If you are looking at adding 10GbE to your network, stay away from the traditional 1GbE architecture and instead look at one of the other two architectures.

- As long as you are looking at either of the 10GbE architectures, consider the port count requirements of each architecture. 10GbE ports are going to be more expensive than 1GbE ports. The converged blade architecture may decrease the number of 10GbE ports that are needed because the number of ports is a matter of bandwidth need.

- If you are going to have any more than a few vSphere hosts, you should seriously consider a 10GbE architecture as a 1GbE architecture is complex and costly to scale beyond a few hosts.

Ultimately, 10GbE architectures will be the default choice as the technology components become more affordable to small and medium businesses. For those that are already versed in Fibre Channel, items like zoning do not change. For those that are familiar with IP-based storage solutions, they can still be leveraged in a 10GbE infrastructure. The knowledge investment can be leveraged in the move to 10GbE. If budget constraints do not allow for a 10GbE architecture from the beginning, a 1GbE architecture is still a great option. 10GbE NICs and switches can be added at a later date as the infrastructure scales beyond the need for two 1GbE switches.

Standard Switching, Distributed Switching, and Third-Party Solutions

Whereas physical network capacity and scalability is mostly about the architectural choices made, logical network capacity and scalability can be affected by the choice of virtual networking that is deployed in the vSphere infrastructure. There are three general options for virtual networking deployment in a vSphere infrastructure:

- **Standard vSwitch (VSS)**—A VMware vSwitch that is configured on a host-by-host basis.

- **Distributed vSwitch (VDS)**—A VMware vSwitch that is configured centrally and distributed across all hosts in a cluster.

- **Third-party virtual switching**—At the time of this writing, the only third-party solution is the Cisco Nexus 1000v. It is a distributed virtual switch.

These different technologies can be implemented in combination with each other, which may be beneficial in certain designs. Before deciding on a virtual switching implementation, it is helpful to have a baseline of the configuration maximums involved with virtual switches. For more information on configuration maximums, please see Appendix A.

A couple of useful maximums to keep in mind are as follows:

- 1016 active virtual switch ports (VDS and VSS) per host
- 256 port groups per host

Today, it would be very unlikely to saturate 1016 active virtual switch ports on any given host. Even if every single virtual machine had ten virtual network cards (the maximum), that would be approximately 101 VMs per host. That is a consolidation ratio that is rarely seen beyond lab environments. The 256–port group maximum means that no more than 256 VLANs can be trunked into each vSphere host. This is a maximum that will likely only be reached in very large organizations or hosting environments. Both of these numbers are still very useful to know so that a range of acceptable ports and VLANs is known. Knowing the configuration maximums can help with infrastructure planning.

So, which virtual switching should be utilized in the virtual infrastructure? The correct decision may be a combination of both standard and distributed (or third-party distributed). The following sections examine the features of the different vSphere switch types and then explore the value that the Cisco Nexus 1000v brings.

vSphere Standard vSwitch

This is the switch type that has been around since the beginning of ESX. It is adequate for network connectivity in smaller infrastructures that do not need advanced features such as port mirroring, QoS, or NetFlow statistics. The following are some of the features that are supported on a standard vSwitch:

- 802.1q VLAN tagging
- Jumbo frames
- TCP Segmentation Offload
- Netqueue
- Directpath I/O
- Load balancing and failover policies for NIC teaming

For the purposes of the capacity discussion, we explore the following features:

- 802.1q VLAN tagging
- Load balancing and failover policies for NIC teaming

The other features mentioned are covered in more detail in the "Networking Performance Management" section.

802.1q VLAN Tagging

Without support for VLAN tagging, a vSphere cluster would not be able to scale beyond a few virtual machines or it would need to be limited to only VMs in the same subnet. The best way to examine the impact of not supporting VLAN tagging is to compare Figure 4.4 and Figure 4.5.

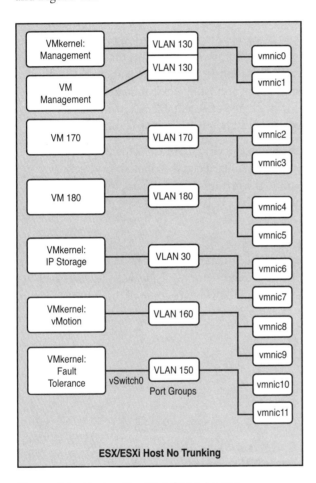

Figure 4.4   Nontrunking Port Group Layout

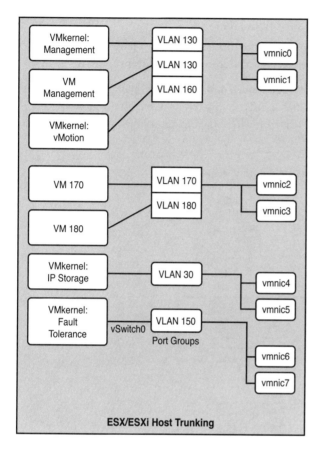

Figure 4.5 Trunking Port Group Layout

Without VLAN tagging, you will be forced to assign physical NICs on vSphere hosts to a specific subnet. This doesn't scale well beyond a couple of VLANs. Even if the infrastructure only had five total VLANs, that would require at least ten NICs per host just for those VLANs if redundancy is to be maintained. With VLAN tagging, the required VLANs can simply be trunked into the vSphere hosts and tagged on specific port groups.

The following sections take a look at some design options with the standard vSwitch.

Load Balancing and Failover Policies for NIC Teaming

The load balancing policies that are chosen for the infrastructure can have an impact on the overall design. The following list reviews the different policies for a standard vSwitch:

- **Route based on originating port ID (see Figure 4.6)**—This load balancing policy uses the originating virtual port ID on the standard vSwitch to determine which uplink will be used to load balance the traffic. This load balancing policy only affects egress traffic.

ESX / ESXi Host – Uplink Chosen Based on Originating Virtual Port ID

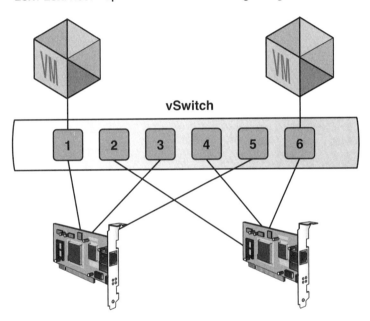

Figure 4.6   Route Based on Originating Port ID

- **Route based on source MAC hash (see Figure 4.7)**—This load balancing policy uses a hash of the MAC address that the traffic is originating from to determine which uplink will be used to load balance the traffic. This load balancing policy only affects egress traffic.

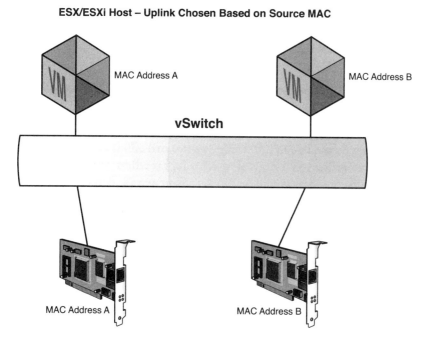

ESX/ESXi Host – Uplink Chosen Based on Source MAC

MAC Address A

MAC Address B

vSwitch

MAC Address A

MAC Address B

Figure 4.7   Route Based on Source MAC Hash

- **Route based on IP hash (see Figure 4.8)**—This load balancing policy uses a hash of the source and destination IP addresses to determine which uplink will be used to load balance the traffic. This load balancing policy is for ingress and egress traffic because it requires help from the upstream physical switches. The upstream physical switches must be configured for EtherChannel for this load balancing policy to be enabled. Sample configurations for etherchannel can be found in VMware KB article 1004048 (see Appendix A for a link).

- **Use explicit failover**—This policy does not actually do any real load balancing. The highest order adapter in the list of active adapters that passes the failover detection criteria will always be used. We usually do not recommend using this policy.

Before diving into the recommendations, the following sections discuss two more options that affect load balancing. Those are network failure detection and failover order. The options are the same for a standard vSwitch and a distributed vSwitch.

Network Failure Detection Options   Following are the network failure detection options with VMware virtual networking.

- **Link status only**—This failure option detects the link status that the physical NICs report on the ESXi host. This protects against things like pulled cables on the upstream switch and power outages on switches. This does not protect against things like configuration errors or cable pulls on the other side of the upstream switches.

- **Beacon probing**—This failure option sends out and listens for beacon probes on the NICs in the ESXi host in addition to link status to determine if a link has failed. This can protect against items such as configuration errors or cable pulls on the other side of the upstream switches.

- **Failover order**

  - **Active uplinks**—An active uplink continues to be used when the network adapter connectivity is up and active.

  - **Standby uplinks**—A standby uplink is only used if one of the active network adapter's connectivity is down.

  - **Unused uplinks**—These uplinks are not used.

Recommendations for vSphere Switches

Following are some recommendations based on our experience with vSphere virtual switches. Third-party switches like the Cisco Nexus 1000v have different policies and recommendations.

- **Recommendation 1: Choose route based on originating port ID for load balancing on a standard vSwitch**—In our experience, the easiest solution is often the best. The route based on originating port ID is the default vSwitch load balancing policy. It does a reasonable job of balancing egress uplinks for the traffic leaving an ESX host. Because this policy uses the virtual port ID of the vSwitch that a VM vNIC is attached to, a VM with multiple vNICs will use different physical uplinks from the ESX host. The "route based on source MAC hash" load balancing algorithm may put those VM vNICs on the same physical uplink depending on how the MAC hash is resolved.

The only true ingress and egress option for a standard vSwitch is the "route based on IP hash" load balancing option. However, we do not recommend using it for most circumstances. Here are some of the reasons why:

- The "route based on IP hash" load balancing option requires added complexity and configuration support from upstream switches. Link Aggregation Control Protocol (LACP) or EtherChannel is required for this algorithm to be used.

- For IP hash to be an effective algorithm for load balancing, there must be many IP sources and destinations. This is because the hash calculation for the source and destination IP addresses for only a couple of IP addresses may turn out to be either both 1s or both 0s. Use the following steps to calculate the IP-Hash.

  1. Convert the source and destination IP addresses to HEX. (There are many IP to Hex converters available online to do this.)

  2. Calculate the modulo over the number of available uplinks in the NIC team.

For example, let's use a NIC team of two physical NICs (0 and 1). Now let's look at a set of source and destination IP addresses for two NFS storage mounts:

VMKnic A = 10.0.0.30 = 0xa00001e

NFS A = 10.0.0.40 = 0xa000028

NFS B = 10.0.0.42 = 0xa00002a

Use the following IP-Hash formula to calculate which uplink it will take.

VMKnic A -> NFS A (0xa00001e Xor 0xa000028 = 36) % 2 = 0

VMKnic A -> NFS B (0xa00001e Xor 0xa00002a = 34) % 2 = 0

To calculate the uplinks using the Windows Calculator, perform the following steps:

1. Change the view to Programmer.

2. Enter the VMKnic A IP in Hex format (a00001e) and click Xor.

3. Enter NFS A IP in HEX format (a000028) and click = .

4. Press Mod, then press 2 because you have 2 uplinks. Then click =. The result is 0.

5. Repeat these steps for each IP for which you want to determine the uplink that will be chosen.

Because both of the resulting IP-Hash calculations resulted in 0, they will both use the first uplink.

For more information on this calculation, please see VMware KB article 1007371 (see Appendix A for a link).

So, unless you plan to calculate the IP-Hash for the IP addresses that you are trying to load balance (which introduces management overhead), you statistically need many source and destination IP pairs for the "route based on IP hash" load balancing option to be effective. Due to the added complexity, the upstream dependency on advanced switch configuration, and the management overhead, we do not recommend the "route based on IP hash" load balancing option. However, if IP-Hash is going to be used, beacon probing should not be used as a network failure detection option.

To review, beacon probing works by sending out and listening to beacon probes from the NICs in a team. If there are two NICs, then each NIC will send out a probe and the other NICs will receive that probe. Because the EtherChannel is considered one link, this will not function properly as the NIC uplinks are not logically separate uplinks. If beacon probing is used, this can result in MAC address flapping errors and network connectivity may be interrupted. More information on this scenario can be found at VMware KB article 1012819 (see Appendix A for a link).

- **Recommendation 2: Choose Route Based on Physical NIC Load when using a distributed vSwitch**—The vSphere distributed vSwitch offers a load balancing option that truly takes the network workload into account when choosing the physical uplink. This is "route based on physical NIC load." We recommend this load balancing option over all the others when using a distributed vSwitch for the following reasons:

    - It is the only load balancing option that actually considers NIC load when choosing uplinks.

    - It does not require upstream switch configuration dependencies like the "route based on IP hash" algorithm does.

    - It may help DRS when it balances the cluster by balancing the uplink load due to new virtual machines being migrated to the host.

    - When "route based on physical NIC load" is combined with Network I/O Control (NIOC), a truly dynamic NIC layout is achieved. More on NIOC is discussed in the "Network Performance Management" section.

Recommended Networking Considerations for vCenter as a Virtual Machine

We recommend deploying vCenter as a virtual machine. That way, the vCenter server itself can take advantage of the benefits of virtualization along with other virtual machines. There is even a new vCenter Appliance that can be used with vSphere 5 for smaller environments. That being said, there are a few considerations when deploying vCenter as a virtual machine.

For larger environments, we recommend provisioning a management cluster to host critical infrastructure management components like vCenter, Active Directory, SAN management, and so on. This isolates vCenter to a separate failure domain so it is easier to troubleshoot any issues with the production cluster.

For small to medium environments, a separate management cluster may not be justified. It is perfectly acceptable to host vCenter on the same infrastructure that it is managing.

We recommend using a VM to host affinity rule to isolate vCenter to failing over to only a few hosts. That way, it is easier to find out which host vCenter is on in the event of a failure.

Let's take a look at some considerations for vCenter when there is a distributed switch in the infrastructure and vCenter is hosted on that same infrastructure. Certain distributed vSwitch operations like virtual machine vNIC static port binding do require vCenter to be online. The following list reviews the binding types on a vSphere distributed vSwitch:

- **Static binding**—A port is immediately assigned and reserved for a virtual machine that is connected to a port group that uses static binding. This happens when you provision a virtual machine. Static binding does need vCenter to be online to function.

- **Dynamic binding**—A port is only assigned and reserved for a virtual machine when it is powered on and the vNIC is in a connected state. The port is then disconnected when the virtual machine powers off or the vNIC is disconnected. The virtual machine must be powered on and off through vCenter if dynamic binding is used. This binding type has been deprecated in ESXi 5.0 and we do not recommend using it with this version of ESXi.

- **Ephemeral binding**—A port is only assigned and reserved for a virtual machine when it is powered on and the vNIC is in a connected state. The port is then deleted when the virtual machine powers off and the vNIC is in a disconnected state. Ephemeral ports can be assigned through vCenter or through ESX/ESXi.

If vCenter is unavailable, then new virtual machines will not be able to be provisioned on the distributed vSwitch with static or dynamic binding. With dynamic binding, virtual machines that are powered on will continue to have network access. With static binding, virtual machines that have been provisioned will continue to have network access regardless of their power state. With ephemeral binding, virtual machines will continue to have network access through the ESX/ESXi hosts even if vCenter is down.

We recommend static binding in almost all circumstances. Dynamic binding is deprecated in ESXi 5.0 and ephemeral binding is operationally slower than static binding. This is because when performing things like virtual machine power operations, ports must be added or deleted with ephemeral binding. Also, any port permissions and controls that are configured on the ports are lost on a power cycle. Ephemeral binding is good in recovery situations where there is a requirement for ports to be bound through ESX/ESXi if vCenter is unavailable.

In designs that have more than two physical NIC ports in the host, a viable option is to put vCenter on a port group located on a standard vSwitch. However, there is no technical reason that this needs to be a requirement. Once vCenter is deployed with static binding, it will always regain network connectivity even if there is an HA failover. Infrastructures with only two 10GbE ports don't really have a choice if vCenter will be hosted on the same infrastructure that it manages. If redundancy is a requirement in these infrastructures, then vCenter will need to be attached to the same distributed vSwitch that it manages. The following process deploys vCenter on the distributed vSwitch:

1. Start with a standard vSwitch on the host.

2. Deploy the vCenter virtual machine on the standard vSwitch.

3. Create the new distributed vSwitch and set up any necessary port groups with static binding (especially the port group that vCenter will be attached to).

4. Move one physical NIC to act as a dvuplink on the distributed vSwitch while still keeping at least one physical NIC as an uplink on the standard vSwitch.

5. Once the network connectivity is verified on the distributed vSwitch, migrate the vCenter virtual machine networking to the distributed vSwitch.

6. Move the remaining physical NICs to act as dvuplinks on the distributed vSwitch.

Cisco Nexus 1000v Distributed vSwitch

The Cisco Nexus 1000v is a distributed virtual Cisco switch that can be used along with or instead of the VMware virtual switches. The value that Cisco brings with the Nexus 1000v is network visibility and management. The networking team in an organization can manage a Nexus 1000v switch with the same methodologies and tools that it uses to manage physical Cisco switches. Let's take a look at the components of the Nexus 1000v.

The Nexus 1000v architecture is similar to a chassis-based Cisco switch. Just like a chassis-based switch, the Nexus 1000v has supervisor modules and line cards. In this case, the virtual supervisor modules (VSM) consist of up to two virtual appliances and the line cards exist as Virtual Ethernet Modules (VEM) that are installed on each ESX/ESXi host that is participating in the Nexus 1000v distributed switch. Each VEM turns the ESX/ESXi host into a line card from the VSM point of view. The VEM is what forwards the traffic while the VSM controls management and configuration. Figure 4.9 shows the components of the Nexus 1000v.

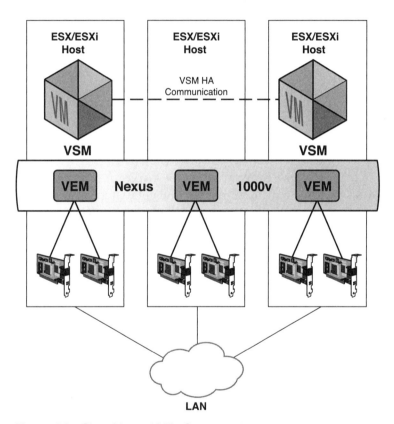

Figure 4.9   Cisco Nexus 1000v Components

From a design standpoint, the same options exist for the Cisco Nexus 1000v as they do for the VMware vSphere distributed vSwitch. We recommend deploying VSMs in an HA pair. We also recommend deploying the Nexus 1000v VSMs outside of the cluster that it is managing. This can be done with the Nexus 1010 appliance. This is a physical piece of hardware that hosts the VSMs.

If the Nexus 1000v will be hosted on the same cluster that it is managing, we recommend placing the VSMs on a standard vSwitch. This is because the VSMs must be up in order to activate a port on the Nexus 1000v and start forwarding traffic. So, by default, when a virtual machine, including the VSMs, power on, the VSMs must be up so they can attach to the distributed switch. If the VSMs are the virtual machines that are powered off, then when they come back up they will not be able to reconnect to the Nexus 1000v because they will not be able to communicate with themselves. This is a chicken-and-egg scenario.

If the Nexus 1000v must be hosted on a cluster that it is managing and there are only two 10GbE ports available on the hosts, there is a way that the VSMs can reside on top of the VEMs that they are managing. Once the VLANs are created, the VLANs that will be used for VSM connectivity must be marked as System VLANs in the Nexus 1000v configuration using the following command:

```
system vlan <VLAN ID's separated by a comma>
```

For example:

```
system vlan 100,101,102,103
```

Any VMkernel interfaces and the vCenter VLAN should also be marked as system VLANs. This tells the Nexus 1000v to always forward traffic and not wait for VSM communication. The process for moving the VSMs to a VEM that they are managing is similar to migrating vCenter to a vSphere distributed vSwitch:

1. Start with a standard vSwitch on the host.

2. Deploy the VSM virtual machines on the standard vSwitch.

3. Deploy the Nexus 1000v configuration on the VSMs and install the VEMs on the ESX/ESXi hosts.

4. Move one physical NIC to act as a system uplink on the Nexus 1000v while still keeping at least one physical NIC as an uplink on the standard vSwitch.

5. Once the network connectivity is verified on the Nexus 1000v, migrate the VSM virtual machines' networking to the Nexus 1000v.

6. Move the remaining physical NICs to act as system uplinks on the Nexus 1000v.

The most useful additions of the Nexus 1000v are the support of access control lists, granular Quality of Service, virtual port-channel support, remote Switched Port Analyzer (SPAN), and more advanced load balancing for NICs in an uplink team. The virtual port-channel support does not even require that the upstream physical switches are Cisco or virtual-port channel capable switches. The Nexus 1000v implements a feature called virtual port-channel host mode (vPC-HM) that is switch agnostic. The Nexus 1000v allows the network infrastructure to stretch into the virtual network. The network team no longer needs to guess what happens to the traffic when it enters the ESX/ESXi hosts.

More information about the Cisco Nexus 1000v can be found in the Cisco Nexus 1000v Data Sheet (see Appendix A for reference).

Performance Management

Many organizations do a great job of capacity management, yet tend to not put as much emphasis on performance management. Performance management can be more difficult because there is more of an unknown factor to determining whether an application is performing poorly. Determining application performance is often a mix of user perception and hard numbers. VMware has many tools to help with performance monitoring and troubleshooting. These are discussed in the following sections.

Storage Performance Management

Storage performance management is just as important as storage capacity management. To reiterate, storage is the only component that touches the entire virtual infrastructure at once. Many environments look at storage planning from a capacity-first perspective. We recommend attacking storage from a performance perspective first, then capacity. This section discusses strategies and tools to help with performance management.

Planning for Peak Utilization

Not all storage arrays are created equal. The array choice for the virtual infrastructure has a big impact on how the virtual infrastructure will scale in the future. The storage is the only resource that is shared by all of the hosts in the vSphere cluster. This means that as the infrastructure scales, there is more pressure on the storage performance than any other component.

Features like array auto-tiering, extra cache, and flash drives can all help with getting the peak performance from the chosen storage. Beyond these features, vSphere also has mechanisms in place to deal with storage performance scaling. Let's take a look at how vSphere can integrate with storage array vendors, then we look at how to manage performance tiers from a vSphere perspective using Storage I/O Control (SIOC).

Storage APIs—Array Integration (Formerly vStorage APIs for Array Integration)

Starting with ESX/ESXi 4.1, VMware has provided storage extension APIs to enable the hardware acceleration of certain storage-related VM operations on VMFS datastores.

These are now known as Storage APIs—Array Integration. On compliant storage arrays, these APIs provide the following benefits:

- Hardware acceleration
- Array thin provisioning

Utilizing the hardware acceleration features on supported storage arrays, the Storage APIs—Array Integration can accelerate the following array operations:

- **Full copy/copy offload**—This allows the storage array to make full copies of certain data within the array instead of having the host read and write the data to the array. This speeds up and reduces the network load when performing the following VM operations:
  - VM cloning
  - Provisioning a new VM from a template
  - Performing a vMotion operation on a VM

- **Block zeroing/write same**—This allows the storage array to zero out blocks of data when providing newly allocated storage so that it can be free of previously written data. This speeds up and reduces the network load when performing the following VM operations:
  - Creating VMs
  - Formatting virtual disks

- **Hardware assisted locking/Atomic test and set (ATS)**—This introduces discrete virtual machine locking on disk sectors instead of SCSI reservations on the entire LUN. Locking occurs on many VM operations, including the following:
  - Migration using storage vMotion (svMotion)
  - Creating a new VM
  - Powering on/off a VM
  - Creating and deleting VMFS datastores
  - Growing a file (think snapshot or a thin provisioned virtual disk growing)

Because more granular locking is enabled by hardware-assisted locking, more VMs can be placed on a single datastore. Also, there is little chance of SCSI reservation conflicts affecting VMFS storage performance. With the Storage APIs, datastore sizes and number of virtual machines per datastore can be chosen more based on business requirements like recoverability and the need for large virtual hard disks instead of technical limitations.

We recommend choosing a storage array that supports the Storage APIs—Array Integration whenever possible if using VMFS. This is especially true if performance scaling is a concern. When discussing NFS-based datastores, the general recommendation is to use 10Gb for NFS connections if performance scaling is a concern. Both VMFS and NFS also support Storage I/O Control. The vSphere Hardware Compatibility List (HCL) can be referenced to see if a particular storage array supports the Storage APIs—Array Integration. See Appendix A for further support for these features.

Storage I/O Control

Storage I/O Control (SIOC) was introduced in vSphere 4.1. vSphere 5 introduced the capability to use SIOC on NFS datastores instead of just VMFS datastores. SIOC becomes more important as the virtual infrastructure is scaled to accommodate more workloads. Let's take a look at how SIOC can help with performance scaling.

To use SIOC, the functionality must be enabled on the datastore. The share and limit granularity is at the VM level. The following are also requirements to utilize SIOC:

- A VMFS datastore can only have a single extent.

- Datastores that use SIOC must only be managed by a single vCenter.

- If SIOC is going to be used with a datastore that is backed by an array that utilizes auto-tiering, check the *VMware Storage/SAN Compatibility Guide* to ensure that the specific auto-tiering array is certified to be used with SIOC.

SIOC introduces the concept of storage I/O shares and storage I/O limits to vSphere storage. As with NIOC, we prefer to use shares only because they provide dynamic performance adjustments in times of contention. Otherwise, all of the virtual machines will have equal access to the storage. Storage I/O shares function in the same manner as NIOC shares, but for storage I/O. The number of storage I/O shares on a virtual machine represents the relative importance of that virtual machine with regard to storage I/O. Only when there is datastore I/O contention, the I/O of each virtual machine is adjusted to the share proportion that each virtual machine has. Limits place an upper limit in IOPS that a virtual machine is allowed to utilize. Limits may lead to wasted resources when there is no contention. So, we recommend utilizing shares only unless it is absolutely necessary to use limits.

Storage Latency and I/O Impact

We want to emphasize that storage can be the most impactful component of the virtual infrastructure. Some storage issues are relatively easy to pinpoint. These tend to be problems like loss of path redundancy, storage processor failures, and HBA or array malfunctions. Performance problems can sometimes be difficult to troubleshoot. There is one general parameter to investigate when performance issues occur. That is latency. Latency refers to the time it takes for a piece of data to travel from one point to another. In this case, from the VMware host to the storage array to be written or from the storage array to the VMware host to be read.

High latency can cause disk timeouts inside of virtual machines, datastore disconnects, and even data loss. It is important to keep an eye on disk latency.

When troubleshooting disk performance, the read and write latency of a particular disk device on a host or the HBA should not exceed around 20ms. In many infrastructures, this latency number will be below 10ms. So, is the disk latency occurring on the VMware host side or downstream in either the fabric or the storage array?

One indicator of host-side latency can be seen when looking at the Kernel read and write latency counters in vCenter for a particular host. Ideally these values should be 0ms but never more than 2ms. If these values are beyond that threshold, then this could point to an HBA queue being saturated. We recommend consulting the array and HBA vendors to determine the optimal command queue depth. If all of the hosts in a vSphere cluster are experiencing high read and write latency on a datastore, then the problem is likely upstream.

One general statistic that can be monitored with an alarm trigger is Virtual Machine Total Disk Latency. The default values for the alarm are to warn at 50ms for 5 minutes and alert at 75ms for 5 minutes. We recommend setting this to something a bit more aggressive like a warning at 15ms and an alarm at 20ms–25ms. Disk bottlenecks such as latency can also be monitored and quickly identified with tools such as vCenter Operations, which is discussed later in this chapter.

Host Performance Management

Host performance management is often overlooked in the beginning of a virtual infra-structure. At the initial implementation, performance might not be noticed as much. As time goes on and more virtual machines are consolidated onto the infrastructure, perfor-mance might suffer if it is not managed appropriately. This section discusses some recom-mendations on managing host resources.

Planning for Growth

We could write an entire book about performance tweaking at the ESX host level for CPU and RAM. There is an abundance of material available on that topic ranging from blog posts to official whitepapers. Here we cover some practical recommendations, based on our experience, for scaling the vSphere host infrastructure from a CPU and RAM perspective as the infrastructure scales. With that in mind, let's start with some resource pool recommendations.

Resource Pool Recommendations

Although it is certainly possible to assign CPU and RAM reservations, limits, and shares to individual virtual machines, we do not recommend this. Per-VM resource controls are an administrative burden and they can affect HA functionality depending on the Admission Control Policy chosen. The Admission Control Policies were covered in Chapter 1, "Laying the Groundwork." They can also make troubleshooting performance issues more difficult.

Even when discussing resource pools, we do not recommend using them until it is absolutely necessary for the workloads or design goals. If resource pools are used, please make sure that all virtual machines are in resource pools at the same level. Do not deploy virtual machines outside of resource pools alongside virtual machines that are in resource pools. Again, this is because resource controls can make troubleshooting performance issues more difficult and there is an administrative overhead associated with using resource pools. If it is not necessary to utilize resource pools, then why introduce them? Resource pools can always be added later.

If resource pools will be used, then we have the following recommendations:

Remember that shares only come into play when there is resource contention.

- Never use resource pools for organization. Resource pools are meant for resource allocation, not organization. We see this quite often, actually. Folders are used for organization.

- Be careful when using resource pools and shares. Shares must be configured and monitored for the amount of virtual machines in a resource pool. Shares provide resources to virtual machines with a priority that is relative to sibling resource pools.

  Let's take a look at two resource pools (see Table 4.2).

Table 4.2 Resource Pools RP-A and RP-B Comparison

Resource Pool	Shares Value	Percentage of Shares	Percentage of Resources per VM
RP-A (15 VM)	"High" (2000)	75%	75 / 15 = 5%
RP-B (5 VM)	"Low" (500)	25%	25 / 5 = 5%

RP-A has a "high" shares value of 2000. RP-B has a "low" shares value of 500. This means that RP-A will have 75% of shares and RP-B will have 25% of shares. Logically, this should mean that virtual machines in RP-A will get more resources than those in RP-B. This might not be the case. Suppose there are 5 virtual machines in RP-B and 15 virtual machines in RP-A. The virtual machines in a resource pool will divide the resources among themselves. The RP-A resource pool will need to divide the 75% of shares among 15 virtual machines. The RP-B resource pool will only need to divide its 25% of shares among 5 virtual machines. This means that the resources will be distributed relatively evenly among all of the virtual machines because RP-A has four times the amount of virtual machines as RP-B. This behavior leads us to the next recommendation.

Never place virtual machines outside of a resource pool on the same level. Virtual machines receive shares based on their hardware configuration. These share values may be greater than the resource pool's share value. This can cause unexpected performance results during times of contention.

We generally recommend not implementing limits on resource pools or virtual machines. This makes troubleshooting performance issues more difficult. Also unlike reservations and shares, a limit is always in place, even when there is no contention. This may artificially throttle opportunities for higher performance when there is no contention.

CPU Recommendations

Although we generally do not adjust many parameters for host CPUs, there are a few recommendations that we will make.

If the host server has AMD-V or Intel-VT hardware-assisted virtualization (most modern systems should), make sure that it is turned on in the BIOS.

Do not use CPU affinity (binding a virtual machine's vCPUs to certain host CPUs) unless the application workload requires it. It limits virtual machine mobility and can adversely affect CPU scheduling for the other virtual machines on a host. Some applications like certain Cisco Unified Communications workloads require CPU affinity to be set for a supported configuration.

If CPU affinity will be used, set the number of physical CPUs to be bound to the number of vCPUs plus one additional physical CPU for processing virtual machine threads like emulated keyboard, mouse, CD-ROM, and so on. For example, if a virtual machine has one vCPU, set the affinity to at least two physical CPUs on the host.

Only assign multiple vCPUs if the application on the virtual machine will truly benefit from multiple vCPUs. The application must be multithreaded to take advantage of more than one vCPU. The reason for this is multiple vCPUs must sometimes be coscheduled by the ESX hypervisor on physical CPU cores. If this happens too often, it may deprive other virtual machines of the CPU resources that they need.

Never assign more vCPUs to a virtual machine than there are physical CPU cores in a host server. For example, if the host had eight cores, 12 vCPUs should never be assigned to a single virtual machine.

Memory Recommendations

There is not much tweaking that you can do to memory itself. There are settings in vSphere 5 that can affect how memory management is handled on the hosts. The following are some of our recommendations.

If space and the design permits, locate the virtual machine swap files on shared storage. This increases the performance of vMotion versus a host-local swap file location. This is because the swap file must be transferred between the source and target host if the swap file is on a datastore that is local to the source host.

vSphere 5 introduced a feature called Swap to Host Cache. This allows a host to swap virtual machine memory pages to a datastore backed by solid-state drive (SSD) before using the virtual machine (.vswp) file. This greatly increases the performance of virtual machine swapping if swapping happens. Use this feature if the hosts are equipped with local solid-state drives. Datastores backed by SAN SSDs should not be used to avoid any network latency associated with swapping to these SSDs.

Although the previous recommendation is a nice safety net for virtual machine memory performance, we recommend that the hosts are sized appropriately for the target consolidation ratio. Do not overcommit production hosts to a large degree. Also, keep an eye on swap activity to avoid performance problems.

Networking Performance Management

In the past, a single host with virtual machines would not even come close to saturating a 1GbE uplink. In most cases, that is still very true today. However, as consolidation ratios become more dense and with the further deployment of 10GbE infrastructure, networking performance management becomes more important. More virtual machines on a single host combined with two-port 10GbE architectures means that performance management is required.

Planning for Growth

Truly dynamic infrastructures with high consolidation ratios will likely use a distributed vSwitch for the advanced features like Load Based Teaming (LBT) and Network I/O

Control (NIOC). These two features combine to create a dynamic networking architecture. This section covers how these two features can be used to manage the performance of a growing virtual infrastructure.

Network I/O Control and Load Based Teaming work together nicely in 10GbE infrastructures. The challenge with 10GbE infrastructures is that there are typically only two 10GbE NIC ports to work with on any given host. Because a best practice is to enable redundancy for different traffic types, all traffic types must travel across the two 10GbE ports in a NIC team. This can be problematic if one traffic type dominates all the other traffic types. Controls must be used to make sure this does not happen. Network I/O Control plays an integral role in controlling the different traffic types.

Network I/O Control allows any given traffic type to use as much bandwidth as it needs as long as there is no contention for bandwidth. In times of contention, the shares value of a specific traffic type will determine how much bandwidth it can use. The shares value will be a percentage of the total number of shares configured on the vSphere distributed switch. Take a look at the following example to gain a better understanding of network shares:

Shares:

- **Management**—10 shares

- **vMotion**—40 shares

- **FT**—20 shares

- **iSCSI**—40 shares

- **Virtual machine**—40 shares

- **Total Shares**—Management (20) + vMotion (40) + FT (20) + iSCSI (40) + Virtual Machine (40) = 160

To see how much bandwidth each traffic type will receive in times of contention on a single 10GbE link, use the following calculations:

NOTE

You can also define custom network resources beyond the default traffic types (FT, iSCSI, vMotion, management, vSphere Replication, NFS, and virtual machine).

Bandwidth:

- **Management**—10 / 160 = .0625 × 10Gb = 640Mbps

- **vMotion**—40 / 160 = .25 × 10Gb = 2.5Gbps

- **FT**—20 / 160 = .125 × 10Gb = 1.25Gbps

- **iSCSI**—40 / 160 = .25 × 10Gb = 2.5Gbps

- **Virtual machine**—40 / 160 = .25 × 10Gb = 2.5Gbps

This represents the bandwidth only in times of contention and only on a single 10Gb uplink. In a NIC team using Load Based Teaming, the workloads will be balanced across the two 10Gb uplinks depending on the NIC load. Although it is possible to also set a limit on a given workload type, we generally do not recommend it as it will limit the traffic even if there is no contention, which defeats the purpose of shares to some degree. Traffic shaping can also be used if more control over ingress traffic is needed.

Network I/O Control combined with Load Based Teaming does a good job of dynamically managing traffic in a 10GbE infrastructure. As 10GbE becomes more common, the benefits of traffic management will become even more apparent. For those who need even more granularity and control from a performance, capacity, and security perspective, there are hardware-assisted controls available like the ones available from the Cisco UCS platform or the HP Blade platform. The Cisco Nexus 1000v is also available to enable more granular control, as discussed in the "Networking Capacity Management" section.

Planning for Peak Utilization

Bandwidth and network performance is not often an issue in a virtual infrastructure. vSphere does have some features that administrators can use to get every ounce of performance out of their virtual networking if it is needed. First, let's look at some general recommendations:

- Always use the latest virtual NIC drivers available for the guest operating system. The highest level of NIC is VMXNET 3. We recommend using this driver in most cases where it is supported.

- Always use the latest hardware version for the vSphere version that is running in the infrastructure. For vSphere 5.x, the latest virtual hardware version is 8.

- Enable jumbo frames for IP storage workloads (iSCSI and NFS). Jumbo frames must be enabled on the vSwitch or a VMkernel interface by setting the MTU to 9000. The upstream switches must also be enabled for jumbo frames. Jumbo frames are also supported inside of certain guest operating systems, but this feature is not used often.

There are also some specific features that you can take advantage of to gain more performance in the virtual network infrastructure. For this discussion, the following sections look at three features:

- TCP Segmentation Offload (TSO)
- Netqueue
- Directpath I/O

TCP Segmentation Offload (TSO)

TSO is a part of the TCP Offload Engine (TOE). The TOE is an integrated circuit on certain NICs that processes TCP headers. Although not necessarily a network performance enhancement, support for TSO can increase overall host performance. Large chunks of data that are sent over the network are broken up into smaller segments. This process is called segmentation and it is often performed by the TCP protocol stack in the host computer. TSO is a feature included in modern network cards. Network cards that are equipped with the TSO can process the segmentation instead of the host computer. This can greatly decrease the load on the host CPU. TSO is enabled by default on VMkernel interfaces and is used on supported guest operating systems that use the Enhanced VMXNET 2 driver or the VMXNET 3 driver.

Netqueue

Netqueue is a technology that can greatly increase the performance of network receive transactions. Netqueue combined with supported network adapters can provide multiple receive queues instead of just one. This means that received packets can be processed by multiple cores in a multicore host. Netqueue allows the network performance to scale along with the CPU performance. Netqueue is supported on certain 1Gb and 10Gb NICs. Netqueue is enabled by default on ESX/ESXi 4.x and greater.

Directpath I/O

Directpath I/O is a feature in vSphere that can allow virtual machines to access physical PCI functions. This means that virtual machines that use Directpath I/O can access NICs directly in an ESX host. This can improve network performance for those workloads that need it. We do not recommend using this for every workload because there are some design considerations. The following features are not available when using the default Directpath I/O functionality in vSphere:

- Hot adding and removing of virtual devices

- Suspend and resume

- Record and replay

- Fault tolerance

- High availability (because there is a physical dependency on the host with Directpath I/O)

- DRS migrations (because there is a physical dependency on the host with Directpath I/O; this means no vMotions)

- Snapshots

These design constraints may be worth the added benefit of extra network performance. It depends on the workload. For those infrastructures that have standardized on the Cisco UCS B-Series platform, Directpath I/O can be utilized without the previously mentioned design constraints. With the Cisco UCS B-Series server platform, it is possible to gain the benefit of Directpath I/O and still use the following vSphere features:

- vMotion

- Hot adding and removing of virtual devices

- Suspend and resume

- High availability

- DRS

- Snapshots

The Cisco UCS B-Series server platform utilizes a Cisco technology called Virtual Machine Fabric Extender (VM-FEX). This technology allows a hardware-based distributed virtual switch to be deployed in the actual Fabric Interconnect components of the UCS. Then a vNIC from the Cisco UCS Virtual Interface Card in the ESX host blade can be assigned directly to a virtual machine. At this point, the switching for the virtual machine is handled directly by the UCS Fabric Interconnects instead of by the hypervisor and a software vSwitch. Figure 4.10 demonstrates the VM-FEX functionality.

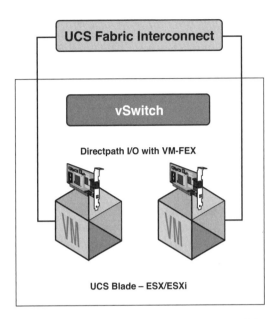

Figure 4.10   Directpath I/O with Cisco VM-FEX

vCenter Operations Management Suite

The recommendations in this chapter have been tactically significant and can help ensure a solid management foundation. As the infrastructure grows and more virtual machines are introduced, a more comprehensive set of tools will be needed to troubleshoot and manage capacity and performance of the virtual infrastructure. VMware's vCenter Operations Management Suite can help with that. The vCenter Operations Management Suite is a suite of software for the virtual infrastructure that has tight integration with vCenter. Because the software is deployed on one or more virtual appliances, the installation and configuration is relatively easy.

The vCenter Operations Management Suite can help with troubleshooting, capacity planning and forecasting, performance management, and even application dependency mapping. The Enterprise Plus licensing level even adds support for third-party management tool integration. At a minimum, we recommend the advanced level of licensing to get the full benefit of the features discussed here.

Troubleshooting

The vCenter Operations Management Suite has the ability to monitor the infrastructure and send out various alerts. Many software suites offer this functionality; however, the vCenter Operations Management Suite uses adaptive algorithms to only send alarms relevant to the infrastructure that it is monitoring. For example, if over time it is normal for a certain virtual machine to constantly use up 90% of its assigned CPU resources, then this will be considered normal behavior that is part of the baseline. If it is not normal behavior, the administrator may be alerted to this behavior. Also, when troubleshooting a particular problem, vCenter events can be correlated to things like performance spikes, as shown in Figure 4.11.

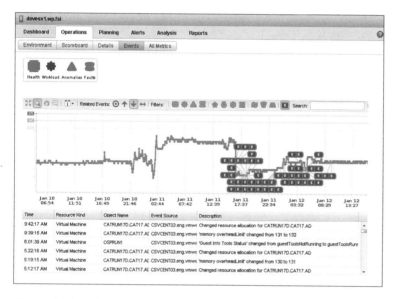

Figure 4.11   vCenter Operations Event Correlation

There is also a Dashboard view so that the administrator can view the overall health of the infrastructure at a glance, as shown in Figure 4.12.

Capacity Planning and Forecasting

The initial capacity planning for a new virtual infrastructure is relatively straightforward. However, as time passes and the infrastructure grows, the business must have a grasp on capacity forecasting. Questions like "When do I need to add more infrastructure resources such as memory, disks, or hosts?" need to be answered. This is where vCenter Operations Management Suite's forecasting component (formerly sold separately as Capacity IQ) shines. It is capable of forecasting when more resources need to be added, as shown in Figure 4.13.

Figure 4.12   vCenter Operations Dashboard View

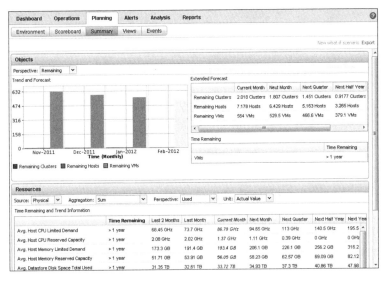

Figure 4.13   vCenter Operations Capacity Planning and Forecasting

This feature also allows the administrator to run reports and manage views to help size the virtual infrastructure on an ongoing basis. An example of this is seen in the Oversized Virtual Machines view shown in Figure 4.14.

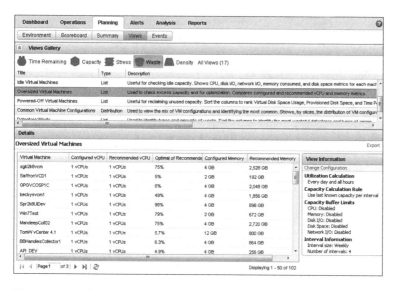

Figure 4.14 Oversized Virtual Machines View

Performance Management

The forecasting feature of the vCenter Operations Management Suite can also help with performance management. If it is shown that the infrastructure will run out of resources soon, the administrator can dig in deeper to see if more resources need to be added or if the existing resources just need to be tweaked. An administrator can get a good look at the overall status of the virtual infrastructure from a capacity and performance view with the Heat Map view, as shown in Figure 4.15.

Application Dependency Mapping

If the Virtual Infrastructure Navigator component (a virtual appliance) is deployed, the administrator can see application dependency mappings between virtual machines. This is especially useful for determining how virtual machine outages will affect three tier applications. An example of this application mapping is shown in Figure 4.16.

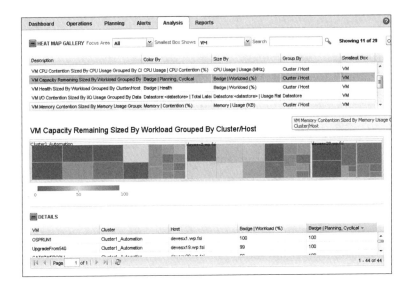

Figure 4.15 vCenter Operations Heat Map View

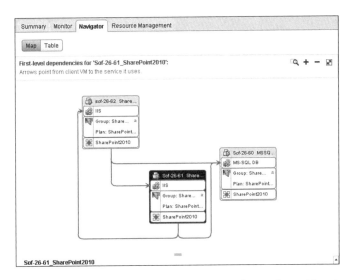

Figure 4.16 Virtual Infrastructure Navigator Dependency Mapping

Managing the Environment Summary

Managing the virtual infrastructure is an ongoing workflow. There are some decisions to be made up front, such as "scale out versus scale up." After that, as the infrastructure grows, vSphere has many features available to help manage the capacity and performance of the design. The recommendations mentioned in this chapter are a mix of VMware best practices and our own field experience. These recommendations can lead to a solid foundation for a dynamic virtual infrastructure that can meet business demands very quickly. Use the features and tools that were mentioned in this chapter as you see fit for your business requirements. We recommend using the findings and reports from tools like vCenter Operations to conduct monthly review meetings for the infrastructure stakeholders. This will help determine whether tweaks need to be made in the infrastructure and when new resources need to be purchased. This can be invaluable in eliminating roadblocks toward a 100% virtual infrastructure. This is discussed in the next chapter.

Chapter 5

Roadblocks to 100% Virtualization

This book began by describing the proper framework for building a solid vSphere infrastructure design. It further discussed the processes for implementing, operating, and managing the design. At this point, you have completed your first foray in virtualization, but there might still be some work ahead. Now it is time to move on to the final frontier—working toward 100% virtualization.

Virtualization is an enabler for higher availability and easier management of servers. In fact, we would go so far as to say that virtualization is the leading cause of scope creep in our customers' projects. Often, engagements start off with a set number of physical servers that will be consolidated. Sometimes before we even get started, that number creeps up as physical hardware begins to fail and hardware reaches its end of life. Many organizations start off deciding to virtualize 60%–80% of their servers or a single location and end up going far beyond their original goals. A VMware vSphere infrastructure certainly makes this easy; however, the last stretch toward 100% virtualization can be difficult. This chapter discusses the many reasons for this difficulty. Although some of the issues that prevent achieving virtualization are technology roadblocks, a majority of the issues are related to political and people constraints.

While discussing roadblocks to further virtualization, this chapter breaks the discussion up into two main types of roadblocks, political and technical.

Political Roadblocks

When discussing the politics of an organization, we refer to many different things. In its simplest form, the politics of an organization is a sum of the organization's people, policies, and culture. This simple equation, though, is very complex. Like people, organizations form their personalities, which affect the way business is done and, ultimately, decisions about technology.

The culture and personality of an organization will vary from organization to organization. Although organizations that share similar lines of business might have a similar culture, they can have differences as a result of the way they grew or their size. For example, an organization that has grown through heavy acquisition will likely be very different than an organization that has grown entirely through its own operations. Similarly, organizations of contrasting sizes will often be very different culturally. Let's continue by talking about some specific areas that affect our end goal of 100% virtualization.

Financial Roadblocks

Before getting into some of the other areas of organizational culture and politics, talking about the financial roadblocks is a good place to start. After all, without the financial backing for further virtualization initiatives, it is likely future projects won't go very far. Being able to substantiate cost savings and a return on investment of current and future projects is very important.

Capex Versus Opex

Capital expenditures (Capex) refer to expenses toward the acquisition of assets such as hardware and software technology. Operational expenditures (Opex), on the other hand, refer to the expenses of operating this environment. The two are very different; however, there is typically a relationship between the two. The relationships, however, can be very deceiving when only looking at the big picture, so let's look closer at a few examples of relationships between capital and operational expenditures. Note that these are just some of the relationships we have witnessed. Not all situations will hold true for every environment. The important thing to understand about capital and operational expenditures is that you must look closely at the situations involved if you are to successfully sell the organization on virtualization. For a further understanding of both capital and operational expenditures, check out the resources listed in Appendix A, "Additional Resources."

An Increase in Opex

An increase in operational expenditures may be done for several reasons. For starters, you might increase operational expenditures to fix an ever-increasing scale of environmental issues or to plan for growth of further technology assets to be supported. This increase can be proactive or reactive.

An increase in Opex may be the result of capital expenditures, or it may even be a measure to reduce Capex. If decreasing capital expenditures is sought, an organization may increase or maintain what appears to be a higher amount of operational expenditures to decrease capital expenditures.

An example of such an increase is leasing hardware versus purchasing. Leases are often considered operational expenses, and companies may choose to lease hardware instead of purchasing for many reasons.

When it comes to virtualization, an organization with this objective will have a hard time entering or continuing with virtualization in some cases. Virtualization requires additional hardware and software purchases, and this might not fit within the organization's plans. Whether it is a sound financial decision to increase operational expenditures at the cost of capital expenditures really depends, though, on the organization. Although it wouldn't be our first approach, if this solves a business's objectives and saves the company more money than a further investment in virtualization, it might be the right decision for them. The important thing is having a good understanding of the decisions and how technology can help improve the company in terms of cost savings as well as potential profitability through enhancements to the business.

When selling this type of organization on virtualization, it is important to show the future benefits of capital expenditures financially. Showing how spending one dollar toward capital expenditures would reduce capital and operational expenditures by two dollars in several years could help a business to rethink this initiative. However, an organization may choose to continue to use its existing hardware at the expense of additional operational expenditures. This will also likely include the acceptance of a greater risk of downtime.

An Increase in Capex

An increase in capital expenditures is often done when investing further in the business. A return from the business is likely anticipated on the investment. This may come in the form of enhanced capabilities that ultimately make the business more money or, in some cases, in the form of a reduction in operational expenses.

When it comes to virtualization, an organization with this objective will likely have an understanding of the benefits of virtualization and how its capabilities help meet business objectives. With the proper capital backing and a well-outlined and executed virtualization implementation, a business can greatly reduce its future capital expenditures and begin to quickly reduce its current operational expenditures. Although in larger environments a virtualization project can pay for itself versus doing a stand-alone hardware refresh, smaller environments will have a harder time justifying the hardware costs of an initial virtualization rollout if they aren't already planning on spending additional money on capital expenditures.

A Decrease in Opex

A decrease in operational expenditures can be the result of an increased investment in capital expenditures that help stabilize and optimize server environments such as a vSphere-based virtualization implementation. Regardless of the cause or the effect, a decrease in operational expenditures almost always results in an increase in capital expenditures.

If an organization decides it will get by with less operational resources, it is going to need technology to perform the work and effort of employees. The problem that often occurs, though, is the same operational knowledge and availability may not exist to solve these problems.

When selling virtualization to this type of organization, it is necessary to show that operational expenses can be reduced, but to also emphasize the skill sets required to be maintained. Additionally, it is vital to emphasize the importance of investing money on hardware and software for virtualization initiatives as well as ongoing training to support the new infrastructure.

A Decrease in Capex

A decrease in capital expenditures can be the result of an increased investment in operational expenditures, as mentioned earlier. One such operational expenditure is the leasing of servers. Another situation where capital expenditures tend to decrease is during times when capital is not available to the organization to spend and as a result, new efforts are not being approached as they were previously. One effect of this is that this can also lead to a decrease in operational expenditures over time.

For example, when new systems aren't being deployed to save money, a repercussion often seen is higher-than-normal turnover of some technology employees who typically like working on new things. Because the organization is operating in a cost-savings mode, the employees will often not be given any reason to stay, nor will their positions be replaced. From the perspective of an IT engineer, this situation is a downward spiral at times as the budgets for capital and operational expenditures continue to diminish. For a business, this may be a necessary action, however, to continue operations.

When it comes to starting or continuing virtualization, these organizations are extremely hard to continue with virtualization objectives. If the hardware is not already there, the ability to invest in new hardware does not exist. When refreshes do occur, they are sporadic, leading to various models and potential incompatibility among hosts to start building a virtualization infrastructure. Operationally, the knowledge and time to properly design an environment does not necessarily exist and even if the hardware is available, environments are often then saturated with resources as sizing has not been properly completed. It is very hard to sell virtualization to an organization that is continually cutting both capital and operational expenditures.

ROI

We talked briefly about capital and operational expenditures and the desires of businesses to control each. More specifically, a business often needs to see the potential return on investment of its solution. Financially speaking, there are many ways to show this and VMware offers the Return on Investment (ROI) and Total Cost of Ownership (TCO) calculator to help financially justify virtualization initiatives.

With the different possible costs of existing capital and operational expenditures on top of the plethora of choices when it comes to future deployments and operations, it is difficult to talk about the subject without going into great lengths. As a result, this section instead focuses on some specific areas of virtualization projects where money is saved or spent. It also talks about some key items virtualization enables and the potential impacts to the business as a result. Some of these have a direct and present financial correlation, whereas others have a less direct and future impact. The former is typically the area of focus and for many reasons, it should be. Future impacts and planning items such as disaster recovery, however, also need careful consideration, and this chapter discusses what virtualization brings to the table in those areas as well.

Where Money Is Spent

Although it might be possible to reuse hardware to start or continue a virtualization initiative, it is more likely that some new hardware will need to be purchased. In some cases, this transformation can be extreme. If an organization never had shared storage and managed networking, a proper design is going to call for redundant managed network switches and a reliable shared storage solution. This can lead to a balancing act of where to spend scarcely available funds. This chapter discusses the prioritization of spending on virtual infrastructure shortly.

In addition to hardware expenditures, new software licensing and maintenance are introduced for both vSphere and any ancillary products used for management or backups.

DEPLOYMENT TIP

If using Microsoft OEM licensing for the existing servers, consider using datacenter licensing for the new rollout. OEM licensing is not transferrable to new hardware and new licensing will need to be purchased.

Where Money Is Saved

Although it is possible to save money immediately, it is more likely the cost savings will take place over time. The rate at which savings will be returned to the business will vary, and savings may be realized immediately, soon after, or years down the line.

As mentioned, there are additional costs involved in terms of software licensing and maintenance; however, consider the items being reduced or eliminated. For each piece of hardware, there is a cost to operate and maintain this hardware, including power and cooling costs, warranty and support costs, and software licensing. Additionally, you also need to consider items such as floor space when colocating, cost of network ports, and UPS use.

The reduction in hardware also brings about future operational and capital expenditure reductions. Additionally, consider the costs of cooling, powering, and having all those physical servers hosted.

Where Value Is Added

Another key area to look at that is harder to quantify is areas where value is added that virtualization enables. Specifically, three areas you should look at are high availability, disaster recovery, and distributed resource sharing.

High Availability

Here, the term high availability is not just the feature of vSphere called High Availability, but also features such as fault tolerance (FT), Distributed Resource Scheduler (DRS), and Storage DRS.

The High Availability feature, along with fault tolerance, provides a feature set that is easy to configure and much more affordable than application and Windows clustering. These features make it affordable for enterprises that formerly could not financially afford the high availability that other clustering technologies provided. Remember High Availability by itself, though, is not the same as application or Windows clustering as a virtual machine is restarted after a host crash. For most applications, this is more than sufficient, though. Additionally, the use of fault tolerance provides for a means of continued application functionality through a replica that is running on another host in Lockstep mode.

Lockstep mode mirrors all operations from the primary virtual machine to a secondary virtual machine.

In addition to conditions where a failure would occur, let's also consider simple firmware and other maintenance. In a nonvirtualized world, host firmware updates would mean operating system downtime. In a virtualized environment, using DRS to migrate virtual machine guests off a host and placing it in Maintenance mode now enables higher uptimes and more flexible maintenance windows. But be aware, items requiring virtual machine downtime such as VMware Tools and virtual hardware upgrades will need to occur.

Disaster Recovery

A proper disaster recovery plan is not something many organizations have today. There are three main reasons for that. For starters, it is not affecting today's day-to-day operations. Second, it is expensive. Third, it is difficult. Depending on the business needs, you have to consider what networks will need to be made available as well as how the data is going to get there or be restored. In some cases, there might be issues deciding where the disaster recovery site will be located.

Virtualization might not fix the issues mentioned earlier, but it greatly helps. By placing all of your virtualized workloads together, you now have the capability to more easily manage a set of resources you are looking to protect. VMware offers Site Recovery Manager, which greatly aids in a recovery plan; furthermore, version 5 now offers vSphere Replication for host-based replication of virtual machines, which is storage agnostic. vSphere Replication is a less-granular approach in terms of recovery points but works great for many organizations. For organizations requiring more granular recovery options and that have the capability to do storage-based replication using their supported arrays, Site Recovery Manager continues to provide great benefits as its prior versions have delivered.

When talking about disaster recovery to your organization, you'll probably realize that it is a hard-selling point in some cases if the budget does not already exist for it. When selling disaster recovery, the biggest two considerations will be how much data the organization can tolerate losing (RPO) and how long the restore of operations can take (RTO). In general, the more static the data, the less important the RPO; the more the business needs to have its systems available, the more important the RTO.

Dynamic Resource Sharing

Earlier we mentioned VMware's feature Distributed Resource Scheduler (DRS) and its ability to assist with High Availability. It is important to note the ability of a vSphere infrastructure to dynamically allocate resources among virtual machines. Servers have continually become more powerful and by default come with way more disk, CPU, and memory than a single workload typically needs. A single vSphere host will do a good job of eliminating wasted space by pooling the resources; however, DRS will provide these benefits across your entire infrastructure of hosts. Its ability to balance the virtual machine load across hosts is not the only capability it has. vSphere 5 now also offers the capability to balance storage loads across datastores, further attesting to its abilities in reducing operational efforts when properly designed and implemented.

Choices for Limited Funding

Financial resources for a project are typically not going to be endless and careful consideration of where to spend money will need to take place if all pieces of a virtualization project cannot be purchased as originally desired. For purposes of this discussion, you should consider three pieces; server hardware, networking, and storage:

- **Server hardware**—In our opinion, server hardware is generally going to be the first place you should look for other alternatives. Regardless of the vendor, your choice in server hardware may be a blade solution or standard rackmount servers. Blade servers are typically going to be cheaper in the long run at scale and for growth; however, it might not be an option to spend the money up front. Additionally, in some environments the number of servers will not warrant the investment in a blade infrastructure. If this is the case, consider the costs involved for a standard rackmount server. Also understand that an investment in a blade infrastructure today also may be an investment in a more resilient infrastructure.

> **NOTE**
>
> Blades are often deployed even when more expensive to provide a more resilient solution that provides for increased availability in the event of failure.

- **Networking**—The next area to look at alternatives and cost reductions is networking. Again being careful here, you need to make sure you have the proper levels of redundancy and throughput in your environment; however, perhaps today is not going to be the day that 10-gigabit networking is brought into the organization. A server with many gigabit interfaces and utilizing the existing redundant gigabit networking might be a better solution for a budget-tight implementation.

- **Storage**—The last area to consider is storage. Storage is typically the piece that is most undersized during a design and is also the part that is usually cut down when it comes time to save money on solutions. We would go as far as to say that in some cases if you are not going to implement a storage solution that exceeds your expected growth, you should consider holding off on the purchase and implementation.

The problem with storage tends to be ignoring or underestimating the need for performance and overestimating the needs of capacity. Further adding to that is the lack of understanding of usable capacity of a storage solution and the impacts of various storage configurations.

If only part of a solution is going to be ordered and other alternatives exist for the rest, purchase the storage as designed in the solution. If a lesser amount of drives can be purchased, ensure that you only virtualize as many workloads as the storage can handle until the additional drives are purchased.

Another change that will save money is going from Fibre Channel to IP-based storage. If Fibre Channel storage is not currently in the environment, this might not be as much of a problem compared with an environment that has already been using Fibre Channel storage. Often disregarded is storage latency, which is most greatly reduced with the usage of Fibre Channel. The argument that 10-gigabit NFS is faster than 8-gigabit FC is not a valid one. 10-gigabit NFS is capable of more bandwidth but has higher latency.

The specific decisions will vary for your environment but the important thing to consider is if the solution is going to meet the needs of your applications.

Policies and Culture

Culture and policies will heavily influence the decisions of an organization's employees. It is important to understand the culture of an organization and the business's objectives. There are many factors of organizational culture that affect technology decisions. A full discussion of these is outside the scope of this book; however, this section discusses some key IT decisions that affect the organization and their roles in preventing virtualization initiatives.

Business-Driven Initiatives

It is important to ask yourself whether the virtualization initiatives are backed and driven by the business. Historically, virtualization begins as a means to facilitate testing and development. This has led in some cases to a misperception of what virtualization can deliver to the business. More important, though, this means the technology is not understood yet by the business's decision makers. Their buy-in for virtualization has not yet taken place and any initiatives are only driven by IT at this time. As discussed earlier in this chapter, understanding a business's goals as well as showing a return on investment is key to selling virtualization to the business and continuing the rollout of the solution.

Roles and Responsibilities

Even if a business has bought in to the benefits of virtualization, there might not be agreement or a cohesive effort to work on the initiatives within IT itself. IT organizations that have departments that operate in silos are a big contributor to the lack of a unified effort in some organizations. We've seen organizations that have four different teams responsible for different virtualization initiatives. This resulted in a lot of people who knew very little about virtualization as well as a lot of money spent on hardware that was barely used.

Even when an IT organization operates under a single organizational unit, similar problems occur. Virtualization touches every layer of an IT organization. Selling virtualization to the business is one thing, but think about the challenge of selling virtualization to the network, storage, and various application teams.

Several years ago, it was commonplace for an application owner to do everything possible to halt the migration of an application to a virtual machine. Today, this is less of a problem, but application owners request some limiting configurations such as virtual machine–based reservations and the assignment of resources that might not be needed.

Before the days of the Nexus 1000V virtual switch, networking teams would ask for further insight into the virtual infrastructure to manage it. Virtualization administrators had little or no knowledge of networking and many times couldn't get the help they needed from network administrators who had little to no knowledge of virtualization. Now that network management exists, many network teams are now trying to own the network piece of a virtual infrastructure. In some organizations, this works well, while in others virtualization administrators are hesitant to give up control of a piece of their infrastructure.

Storage administration traditionally had very little to do with the networking teams and server teams. When the server team did need storage, they asked for a set amount of storage to be presented and they were on their way. With virtualization introduced, the requests became a little less standard—and simply asking for a set amount of storage was not enough. Virtualization administrators began to need to know more about the storage the virtual machines were being put on. With the introduction of IP-based storage, the network and storage teams needed to begin working closely with each other for the first time.

With these relationships so new, disagreements about the best way to implement a component or proceed with an implementation halt and prohibit many implementations even today. It is still not understood in many organizations why a single server might need six or more gigabit network interfaces or why a single LUN for storage needs to be available to many hosts and be backed by more than a five-disk, RAID-5 volume.

Some organizations will need to continue to operate with disparate roles as a result of their size or need for specific skill sets; however, knowledge transfer needs to take place. Whether an individual is a specialist or a generalist, today's virtualization administrators require a skill set that blends roles that were formerly spread out in most organizations.

Today's Virtualization Administrator

In the early days of virtualization, an administrator was typically deep in understanding of Windows and server hardware. Today's virtualization administrator needs to not only understand servers and vSphere, but also needs to firmly understand many other roles. In some organizations, roles have shifted and a virtualization administrator is also responsible for datacenter networking and for having a firm understanding of storage.

Networking has continued to grow as a required skill set. Developments in IP-based storage have largely driven this need. Additionally, the introduction of converged networks carrying both Fibre Channel and IP protocols has driven the need for an understanding of networking in the datacenter.

Storage has been closely tied to virtualization administration for some time now in many organizations. A deep knowledge of storage as well as the ability to administer and design solutions is a requirement of today's virtualization administrators. Virtualization is, for obvious reasons, a storage-intensive initiative and having unified roles or a solid working relationship between teams is crucial for continued virtualization initiatives.

In addition to the technology skills previously mentioned, it is important to note that individuals who are responsible for such a vital part of the organization's infrastructure need to understand the business's goals and requirements. In larger organizations, this might not be as critical in places where an entire team manages just SQL, but in smaller organizations where only a few people support technology for an organization, this is vital. These individuals tend to be much more a part of the business decisions and their ability to gather and relay information regarding virtual infrastructure design is critical to their success.

Technical Roadblocks

When discussing technical roadblocks to virtualization, there are many areas that commonly hinder virtualization initiatives. It is important to note that the line between political and technical issues might or might not exist in all areas. For example, this section discusses VM sprawl from a technical perspective and is driven by information technology engineers; however, many of its causes are political.

VM Sprawl

The abundance of single-purpose physical servers in organizations helped to demand virtualization technology. In some cases, these servers were seldom used and running on top of hardware that the operating system and applications were not even capable of taking advantage of. Today in many virtualized organizations, the same type of sprawl has occurred and for several reasons. VM sprawl is a roadblock to virtualization initiatives because it takes away resources from other current and future virtual machines. As a result, it causes issues in deployed infrastructures and prevents further efforts to virtualize physical systems.

Virtual servers are easy to deploy. If you have templates configured in your environment, the time it takes to bring up a new server is minutes or hours instead of weeks and months. This has led to the creation of many virtual machines that are either seldom used or in many cases left around after they are no longer needed.

Virtual servers are also hard to get rid of. Technically, it is just a few clicks of the mouse; however, if virtual machines aren't properly tracked, it is hard to know when to decommission them and who owns and uses the systems and applications. In many organizations, the biggest reason for virtual servers being left behind is that they aren't taking up physical space or, in many cases, even being tracked as an asset. Asset tracking in the traditional sense has focused on tracking servers as a physical entity. Regardless of your system, it is important to ensure you can account for what virtual machines are running on what set of vSphere hosts and the underlying storage. This is important not only as you track hardware for upgrades but also for maintenance activities to ensure a change's impact can be properly understood.

If you currently do not have any controls in place to track your environment, you can begin taking action with the following steps:

- Identify ownership of the systems and applications from a technical standpoint.

- Identify ownership of the systems and applications from a business-owner perspective.

- Identify users of the system and its applications.

- Identify systems that are no longer needed.

- Identify systems that are underused and may be consolidated together.

Identifying ownership of the systems and applications from a technical standpoint is your first step in understanding the requirements of the virtual machines in your environment. This might be more difficult in some instances; however, it is a necessary step in understanding the virtual machine's usage in the environment. Additionally, it is necessary to identify the users of the systems. In some instances, application and server owners themselves do not always understand the needs of their users. Before decommissioning any systems, having an understanding of its actual usage is necessary.

Only after you know the owners and users of servers can you identify what systems are no longer needed or can be consolidated together. When thinking about consolidating servers together, understand the impacts of the decision. For example, a common case for consolidation is database servers. Although these may be running separately today, consider the impacts first of running them together. Separate database servers provide for isolation but may lead to more resource utilization. Additionally, consider the necessary availability of systems. You certainly would not want to mix test and development workloads with production as test and development systems will likely be reconfigured and rebooted often.

Additionally, the following are some other points to consider:

- Is running the applications side by side supported?

- Does running databases together make sense from a support and ownership perspective?

- How will upgrades occur for an operating system with multiple applications?

VM Sizing Guidelines

In addition to considering if all those virtual machines that are deployed in your environment are needed, consider if the resources they have are actually needed. This exercise is great for two reasons. For starters, it aids in recovering resources for virtual machines deploying in your environment going forward. Second, it also identifies virtual machines that are using all of their current resources and facilitates adding new resources to those systems to avoid further or future problems.

As discussed earlier in this book, vCenter Operations is a great solution and will assist in virtual machine sizing by getting a baseline on your current environment and continually working to manage and optimize your virtual machines. For those who do not have the product licensed or installed, you may also consider looking at the following areas to properly size the virtual machines in your infrastructure.

Virtual Machine Memory and Processor Configuration

When considering the proper configuration for memory or CPU, assess the performance of your system over a month-long period to discover how much of each of these resources the virtual machine is using. An engagement such as a Capacity Planner delivery is a great way to find out average usage as well as peak usage for each of your physical or virtual workloads.

After analyzing your systems, you might find that many are not using nearly any of their resources and some perhaps are using much of their resources. Consider downsizing memory or processors as needed to fit your environment.

It is difficult to suggest the right configurations for your virtual machines and applications; however, we do have some general recommendations that will help in properly sizing virtual machine memory and CPU configurations.

Make sure you have documented the configuration before any changes are made. Additionally, have a baseline of the performance of the system and applications. This is not only to be able to undo what has been done, but also to understand if there is any noticeable improvement when upsizing or degradation when downsizing.

Additionally, understand if the application and operating system can handle the current or future configuration. Some applications can't use more than one or two CPUs and some operating systems can only handle a certain amount of memory. Ensure you are within those constraints as additional resources can go wasted.

> **TIP**
>
> When changing a virtual machine from a single processor to multiple processors or vice versa, ensure you update the hardware abstraction layer (HAL) when using Windows 2003 or earlier.

Virtual Machine Storage Configuration

When thinking about storage configurations of virtual machines, you need to consider storage from both a size-usage and resource-usage perspective. Again, a performance and utilization assessment will help reveal this information. When thinking about data usage, you can consider thin provisioning to ensure you aren't using any more storage than you actually need. This can be configured on the storage itself or done per virtual machine disk for each virtual machine. Regardless of where it is done, it is important to also understand that this could lead to a situation where datastores fill up if you don't have enough back-end storage to facilitate the growth in your environment. When using thin provisioning, be extra careful to ensure you are alerting from the storage and virtual machine side as data stores are growing toward capacity.

> **TIP**
>
> When using thin provisioning, make sure not to use traditional disk defragmentation. Defragmentation over time causes thin disks to be filled out. Consider using some of the many solutions for defragmentation specifically designed for vSphere environments.

You should also evaluate thick provisioning for each of its use cases. If a system has a larger-than-necessary drive configured and it is configured as Thick, it will certainly waste storage that could be used for other servers and applications. Ensure that drives are properly sized at a virtual machine level and that thick provisioning is used where necessary only. It is our recommendation that you thick provision all operating system volumes as well as any drives containing transactional data such as database applications.

When considering storage performance, make sure your virtual machine disks are placed on the appropriate type of storage. Test and development applications should be separated out and placed on slower storage than production systems. Your most critical applications should be considered for the storage that is not only the fastest, but also the most protected and available.

Application Roadblocks

Applications and their owners have traditionally been one of the bigger roadblocks to virtualizing systems. It was common just several years ago for vendors to refuse to support their application when virtualized—once they noticed the VMware logo in the right corner of the taskbar. Although that issue does still exist today, it is more often a question of technical constraints that make it difficult to virtualize certain applications. The remainder of this section describes a few of these items.

Real-Time Applications

Real-time applications are the next frontier virtualization has been looking to tackle. To date, there are still many real-time applications that we do not recommend virtualizing. The higher demanding, real-time applications may require less than 20ms latency and in the case of stock-trading applications or similar applications, demands could result in huge monetary losses. The real-time applications that are extremely sensitive to latency are often referred to as hard real-time applications.

Some other applications that require low latency, but to a much less-critical degree, are often referred to as soft real-time applications. Today, virtualizing hard real-time applications is not recommended; however, the soft real-time applications—those that can tolerate some latency—can be virtualized when following the proper guidelines.

Whereas ESX 3.5 and prior was not built for real-time applications, vSphere 4 and above have been built to support real-time applications through a redesigned scheduler. Real-time applications are very different from all the other workloads that may potentially exist in a virtualized environment. Real-time applications have high requirements for guaranteed resources, which greatly contradicts the goals of virtualization. Although waiting is tolerable in terms of a print server, it can be detrimental in trading or medical systems where milliseconds of latency can cause the loss of large amounts of money or lives.

Voice Applications

The most widely spread real-time application that is being virtualized in many organizations today is voice. Although the virtualization of voice applications is now possible, some technical roadblocks had to be overcome and, as such, there are specific requirements for deploying voice applications based on vendor supportability.

To keep the latency low, voice applications are typically deployed with dedicated resources. This is accomplished through the use of reservations as well as CPU affinity. CPU affinity reserves a processor core or cores for use by a specific virtual machine only. In addition to dedicating the resources, the virtualization of voice has been enabled by advancements in technology. The support of hardware assist and EPT/RVI memory management assist has both been critical to the ability of systems to handle the needs of applications requiring low latency. The VMXNET3 virtual machine network adapter has also been critical to the virtualization of voice application, providing a paravirtualized network adapter that has improved network throughput to and from virtual machines. Additionally, the release of the Intel Nehalem chipset with Extended Page Tables (EPT) has shown five to six times better performance, further aiding the virtualization of voice and other real-time applications.

As discussed, soft real-time applications are those that can tolerate 20ms of average latency. In terms of voice applications, this also holds true, with worst-case latency of 100ms possible for most solutions.

When determining a solution for voice applications, it will likely be necessary for you to work directly with the vendor to order the necessary hardware so that the solution will perform and be supported. In general, you need to follow the guidelines in the following sections for virtualizing voice applications. Note that some of these recommendations for voice are opposite for those of non-real-time applications.

Dedicate CPU and Memory Resources

We recommend dedicating CPU cores through the use of CPU affinity where required and configuring CPU and memory reservations per the vendors' requirements. Often, as is the case with a Cisco voice solution, the virtual machines will be deployed as an OVF template, which takes care of the reservations. You still may have to modify these settings depending on the virtual machine being deployed and the number of users in your environment. Be aware that using CPU affinity has an implication on the implementation. Please refer to Appendix A for a reference to the potential impacts of CPU affinity on your infrastructure.

Additionally, many vendors also require that you do not overallocate memory resources. This is another attempt to reduce latency as much as possible for the voice applications. The amount of vRAM plus overhead may not exceed the total memory of the physical host.

DEPLOYMENT TIP

When configuring CPU affinity, leave core 0 unused for optimal performance of the host. This core is used by the scheduler and sharing it with a processor-intensive application is not recommended.

Dedicate Physical Resources

Isolate physical resources for the use of voice applications. Real-time applications like voice have different requirements than non-real-time applications. These applications also place different constraints on your environment as a result. For example, the use of CPU affinity prevents those virtual machines from participating in a DRS cluster. When using CPU affinity, be aware that you cannot overprovision CPU resources and the number of cores assigned must be less than the total number of cores. Also be aware that when CPU affinity is configured and a virtual machine is moved from one host to another, the configuration of CPU affinity can be lost when moving between systems that have differing CPU counts.

Use Supported Hardware

Ensure your hardware is supported by the vendor from top to bottom. The virtualization of voice is still very new and vendors require very specific hardware to do so. Use a system with a CPU capable of handling voice virtualization. Use a chipset that supports Hardware MMU assist. For Intel, this is called Extended Page Tables (EPT), or for AMD, this is called Rapid Virtualization Index (RVI).

Use Appropriate Storage

Use adequate Fibre Channel or local storage to avoid any issues with latency. Any delays in disk processing time will be passed along to the application and will result in a low quality of service. Although we wouldn't typically recommend local storage for many instances, remember that today voice applications are often prohibited from participating in a DRS cluster and are often configured with CPU affinity to dedicate CPU cores to the application. Instead, redundancy in many solutions is configured through multiple application servers with primary and secondary virtual machines physically separated.

At the virtual machine level, it will likely be recommended by your vendor to use thick provisioned disks. This is, again, a requirement by vendors to reduce any potential latency to the application. Additionally, it is recommended that you do not overprovision disks even if you decide to thin provision.

Use Appropriate Networking

When thinking about the required amount of bandwidth for voice, there are several factors to consider, including the code being used and bitrate. A full discussion of this is beyond the scope of this book, but the important thing is to understand how much bandwidth should be available per call as well as the number of calls you expect during peak usage.

Where possible, separate network connectivity for voice workloads should be used to provide adequate throughput and availability. For example, let's consider you are using a rackmount server that has six NICs installed, four of which are dedicated to the virtual machines. If you have four separate voice applications configured, consider an active/standby setup for each of the virtual machines. By placing them each in separate port groups and alternating active NICs, with the others serving as standby NICs, you guarantee throughput as well as redundancy when needed.

Growing the Environment

When expanding the environment, add additional servers instead of resources to existing servers. It is very important with voice to scale out and not up, as any potential resource contention increases the latency of the applications.

Troubleshooting Virtualized Voice

When troubleshooting voice issues, the first target should be verifying the infrastructure meets the requirements of the solution. Paying close attention to the vendor requirements, verify whether the amount of resources covers the number of users in the environment. Verify whether the systems are not highly utilized in memory, CPU, or disk and ensure network throughput is adequate. Additionally, you need to verify that packets are not being dropped in your environment through esxtop.

Another issue that can occur is slow TCP performance. This typically affects hosts that have been upgraded. To fix this issue, you need to disable Large Receive Offload (LRO) on each vSphere host. To do this, you need to do the following:

- Log in directly to the host or through the vSphere Client.

- Go to Host, Configuration, Software and choose Advanced Settings.

- Select NET, and change the following from 1 to 0:

  - Net.VmxnetSwLROSL

  - Net.Vmxnet3SwLRO

  - Net.Vmxnet3HwLRO

  - Net.Vmxnet2SwLRO

  - Net.Vmxnet2HwLRO

- Reboot the host.

Business-Critical Applications

Several years ago, many organizations were hesitant to virtualize their most critical applications; however, since the release of vSphere 4 and virtual machines supporting up to 8 vCPU and 255GB of RAM, many organizations have begun and completed the virtualization of their most critical systems. There are two main reasons organizations have either not virtualized their tier-one applications or not completed doing so.

For starters, the concept of virtualization is still not understood by many. As a result, there is a lack of confidence and firm understanding within the business of the values it presents. Even today, some organizations still view virtualization as the IT engineers test and development setup.

Second, virtualization efforts may have been attempted for the business-critical applications but did not succeed. This most often is the result of improperly sizing the infrastructure for the applications. Improper sizing tends to happen both in under- and overprovisioning of resources. Administrators unfamiliar with the repercussions often start out aggressive and overallocate resources. They configure four CPUs when the application only supports two, they configure 8GB of RAM when only 2GB of RAM is needed, and they carry over the physical server's configured storage and give virtual machines large hard disks. Additionally, they often misunderstand the use of resource pools and reservations. The combination of the two leads to resources drying up very quickly.

When resources dry up, these same administrators will start provisioning based on what is available. New virtual machines have one CPU when they need multiple, not enough memory, and too little storage. These same machines if part of a resource pool will by default have less resource shares. In the end, everything ends up performing slowly.

With these tier-one applications, one thing we often recommend is considering if they need to be part of their own cluster. Consider that the rest of your business's applications may tolerate significant amounts of downtime while these other applications need to be

available at all times. They are likely going to also have very different resource requirements in terms of CPU, memory, network, and storage. Lastly, think about the case if you
have already virtualized a majority of your noncritical applications.

Case Study

You have an existing infrastructure consisting of five vSphere hosts that are in a cluster and
are licensed for vSphere Standard. The business would like to virtualize its most critical applications and is prepared to spend the money necessary to add additional hosts and to upgrade hardware where required.

Let's assume the current cluster has hosts that on average are using 50% of their CPU
resources and 60% of their memory. The hosts are configured consistently with 24GB of
RAM and two quad-core processors. Let's also assume the virtual machines have all been
properly sized with no room for the reclamation of resources.

The business-critical applications vary in requirements. Four of them require 8GB of RAM
and four CPUs, while four others use 16GB of RAM and two CPUs. Assuming you could
upgrade the host to 32GB of RAM, what would you do?

There are several things to consider in a situation like this. For starters, is fault tolerance
(FT) a requirement for the business-critical applications? If it is, you need to clarify further
if the existing hosts have CPUs that even support FT. If they do, you also need to ensure
you have dedicated and redundant networking for FT.

DEPLOYMENT TIP

At the time of this publication, fault tolerance (FT) only supports single-processor virtual
machines. Keeping virtual machines in lockstep copy is a network-intensive process that will
be overcome in the near future with the infiltration of 10-gigabit networking.

Another consideration here is licensing. You are currently licensed for vSphere Standard,
which entitles you to 32GB of vRAM entitlement. This will cover you for any virtual
machines configured for the existing setup, but if you choose to upgrade the memory,
you'll need to upgrade your licensing. Additionally, standard licensing does not include
fault tolerance or Distributed Resource Scheduler (DRS), both critical features to have
when virtualizing business-critical applications.

With the information you have, you know the existing infrastructure could be upgraded to
meet the needs of the business today but may not leave adequate room for future growth.
You also run the risk of not having the proper slot size to handle these bigger virtual

machines. The business-critical systems in this case consist of two sets of machines, one of which has large memory footprints and the other of which has large CPU footprints. With hosts that have only 32GB of RAM and eight processor cores, virtual machines with 16GB of RAM and those with four processor cores can cause significant resource contention issues as well as issues with proper balancing and placement.

With all of these considerations, it may be best to order new hardware that is sized to meet the needs of the applications. These hosts should have bigger memory and processor capabilities and be licensed for the advanced features of vSphere through Enterprise or Enterprise Plus that these business-critical applications will make most use of.

Another consideration not yet discussed is storage. Although you need to ensure you have adequate storage space, these business-critical applications will likely require higher performance than typical systems. They also will potentially require higher levels of redundancy. Ensure the existing storage environment meets the business's objectives for performance and availability before mixing differing systems within the same storage array. When using the same storage array, ensure critical virtual machines are not only given adequate storage in terms of performance but also that the storage being presented is being backed by separate physical disks.

As discussed earlier in this book, the success of any virtualization initiative, including those to virtualize the most critical business applications, begins with a solid foundation. No matter what the application is, understanding the application's and business's requirements and designing around them helps ensure a solid infrastructure.

Desktop Virtualization

This chapter talks about the ideas of striving toward 100% virtualization. Desktop virtualization may also be part of your virtualization strategy and it is worth discussing desktop virtualization and its impacts on virtualization initiatives.

Desktops have a much different footprint and demands on the environment than servers. There are also many use cases for desktop virtualization. You may be virtualizing high-end power users who do graphical work or your regular office workers. You may also be virtualizing lab or kiosk PCs. These PCs could range from being in constant use to only being used occasionally. Understanding the target group of users to be virtualized is the first part to a successful View deployment.

Second, once you know who the target users are, dedicating the proper resources to the project is vital. It is our recommendation you install your View desktops on different physical hardware. This is typically much cheaper as licensing for View desktops is all inclusive. Additionally, in a typical View environment, you can install eight to ten View virtual machines per core assuming adequate memory and storage exists.

Memory is another important thing to consider. Your choice to configure 2GB of RAM versus 4GB of RAM not only potentially impacts the amount of memory your servers will need to have, but also the amount of storage you need. Although this holds true for servers, it is often not thought of during designs; however, it doesn't typically end up affecting projects because of scale. A 4GB .vswp file for 50 virtual servers will only utilize 200GB, while that same organization may have 1,000 virtual machines at 4GB utilizing a total of 4TB.

In addition to the concerns of memory configuration on storage usage, you need to carefully consider sizing the environment for performance needs. View allows the creation of linked clone virtual machines that allow huge space savings for virtual desktop infra-structures. It is not uncommon to only need a handful of disks to design a View solution for size and redundancy but need trays of disks to properly account for performance needs. As a result, View is a great case for the use of flash-based storage. Placing operating system disks for linked clone virtual machines on flash-based storage and user data on slower storage in many cases is cheaper than traditional storage.

Knowing your available network bandwidth and latency when doing remote View desktop deployments is necessary more than any other product. It is also one that needs to be thoroughly piloted before being brought into a production environment. The pilot needs to be specifically targeted toward the prospective users and not just individuals testing the product. For example, if you test users who work in Microsoft Office all day with a single monitor, but end up deploying the product to individuals who regularly view media and have three monitors, you will likely fail to deliver an acceptable result. Similarly, you must know your protocol. If you are going to be deploying PC over IP (PCOIP)-based thin clients but are testing with Remote Desktop Protocol (RDP), you will notice much worse performance.

Finally, understand what each user is going to require from the network in terms of both average and peak utilization. As just mentioned, the number of monitors has an impact on the amount of bandwidth needed; in fact, it is a multiplying factor for each monitor added, so a dual-monitor user will require twice the bandwidth of a single-monitor user. Users who regularly view audio or video have much greater requirements than general office users. Also understand that what you are designing needs to scale, so know what each user type is going to cost you in terms of network bandwidth and storage utilization. More resources on deploying a virtual desktop environment can be found in Appendix A.

The Future of Desktop Virtualization

Some technology leaders, including VMware's own CEO Paul Maritz, have stated we are now entering the post-PC era. In these new times, the need to have what is thought of as a typical computer will continue to wane while users continue their demand for mobile technologies that allow them to accomplish everything they could on their computer but easier. It will be easier because the devices will be smaller, can be used anywhere, and the experience will be optimized for touch and the device.

The era we have entered also sees more individuals than ever demanding the use of their own devices, both computers and phones. This has been nearly impossible to allow in previous times with the inability to both properly secure and support the devices due to organizations not owning them. With technologies like the ones discussed in the following sections, these concerns are minimized and in some cases eliminated entirely.

While VMware View when used in conjunction with certain apps on mobile phones and tablets today provides a virtual desktop experience that matches the use of the desktop, there is still a gap that exists in making this seamless and easier to use than a computer itself. VMware has developed two new technologies that will soon be fully released in the form of VMware Horizon. VMware Horizon is made up of two distinct products, VMware Horizon Application Manager and VMware Horizon Mobile.

VMware Horizon Application Manager

VMware Horizon Application Manager provides a centralized interface to manage and deploy applications to users, independent of the type of and number of devices the user has. It accomplishes this through application packaging using an existing product, VMware ThinApp. Application Manager allows for easier management as well as security and provides an intuitive graphical interface for users to launch the applications.

As some background, VMware ThinApp is an agentless application virtualization solution that allows the packaging of software into a single executable that can be isolated from one another and the operating system itself. This provides great management benefits and a reduction of support costs, but its most greatly utilized feature is the ability to package applications that will only run on Windows XP and use them on Windows 7.

VMware Horizon Mobile

VMware Horizon Mobile offers organizations the ability to offer, secure, and manage applications to employees' mobile devices. Employees will be able to choose their device and organizations will be able to configure a virtual work phone to be used to access secured applications.

VMware Project Octopus

In addition to how Horizon Application Manager and Mobile allow anywhere access to applications, VMware also is developing another product that allows seamless access to files. Currently labeled Octopus, this service provides secure access to files from any device, allowing users to share and collaborate on files from within and outside an organization. The service will be usable from either an internal infrastructure (i.e., a private cloud) or a public cloud provider.

Storage and Network Virtualization

Virtualization is not just about the operating system or applications. Many technologies are available that virtualize components of storage, networking, and even hardware itself. Now more than ever, these technologies are looking to improve upon themselves using the concepts of virtualization. Although a full discussion of these topics would warrant a book for each, a few things are worth mentioning regarding each.

Storage Virtualization

Virtualization is not new to storage. In fact, SAN-based storage by design is virtualized to effectively abstract the storage from the array and present it to a server or set of servers. Today, this is being taken even further with arrays that are taking more and more responsibility for ensuring the data itself is located on the most appropriate storage, balancing usage and performance. These technologies continue to develop, whereby the type of storage being added is of less and less concern to the storage and virtualization administrator.

Additionally, many types of arrays now have the capability to present other types of storage through them. This is of great benefit as other vendors' systems can now be presented through the existing methods to help reduce the administrative burden of a fragmented environment.

A full discussion of storage virtualization is outside the scope of this book; however, we highly recommend Mostafa Khalil's book, *Storage Implementation in vSphere 5* for an in-depth discussion of storage technologies.

Network Virtualization

Virtualization is not exactly new when it comes to networking. In fact, virtual LANs (VLAN) have been around for some time now, effectively isolating systems into differing broadcast domains even when plugged into the same set of switches. Further developments continue to take place as virtualization has become the norm in organizations.

Although networks were designed under the ideology of systems being plugged in directly to access ports, today's network infrastructure is not that simple. A lot has changed with virtualization. Servers are no longer a static entity in terms of their placement on the network. In the early days of virtualization, even virtual servers would typically make their way back to the network through the same network interface consistently, but with the introduction of clustering technologies, this quickly changed. Today, it is not just about moving from interface to interface but also from site to site.

The Cisco VNTag is a standard proposed by Cisco to address both network awareness and control of virtual machines. It accomplishes this by an additional header into the Ethernet frame, allowing identification of the virtual interface of the virtual machine. Traditional switches do not support forwarding frames where the source and destination MAC are on the port. This means that two virtual machines connected to the same port cannot forward frames with each other on a traditional switch.

A full understanding and discussion of networking virtualization is outside the scope of this book. We recommend checking out some of the resources in Appendix A for those looking to gain a further understanding of the concepts mentioned.

Roadblocks to 100% Virtualization Summary

This chapter talked about some of the many reasons organizations stall in the efforts to virtualize. It is not uncommon to get off the ground running but later become halted for many reasons. Many times, these reasons are purely political and other times they are the result of technical issues. In the real world, there likely is not much differentiation between the two as technical issues can be the result of political issues and vice versa. Although it might not be possible to virtualize your entire infrastructure like the title of this chapter indicates, vSphere provides a framework for you to do so for all of your applications, including your most critical ones.

Chapter 6

Full Case Study

Our goal in writing this book has been to arm you with some considerations and best practices when designing, implementing, operating, and maintaining a vSphere infrastructure. This chapter is all about using this knowledge to discuss a case study. In this chapter, you look at a customer scenario and some of the choices available and justifications for specific decisions made along the way. Let's dive right in to the customer scenario.

Customer Scenario

Crookston and Stagner Bank is a regional bank located in Richmond, Virginia. Your consulting firm has been called to assist with a datacenter refresh project. You have the role of lead engineer on this project. The CIO of Crookston and Stagner Bank has indicated that he would like to explore the benefits of virtualization in this project as the bank has yet to virtualize any of its workloads. The following are some additional questions that were asked during the customer interview along with the answers:

Q: What are your growth plans in the next couple of years? Does the bank plan to stay relatively static?

CIO: We are actually in an acquiring mode this year and for the next couple of years. Part of the push for this datacenter refresh is to prepare the bank for growth, both organically and through acquisition.

Q: Will you need to adhere to any new regulatory requirements as a result of your planned growth?

CIO: Yes, actually. When the bank grows to a certain size, we have to meet new requirements. One of the things that we will be audited for in the next few months is our disaster recovery plan.

Q: Do you have a disaster recovery plan in place today?

CIO: Yes, for our core processing. It is on a hosted platform and the provider takes care of our disaster recovery. For our other workloads, we only have local disaster recovery and even then we only have tape backup. We are looking for something a little more comprehensive and I have heard that virtualization can help us realize greater disaster recovery benefits.

Q: You mentioned tape backup. Do you have the leeway in this project to explore other backup options?

CIO: Yes, as long as they make sense and align to our primary goals, which are consolidation through virtualization and a more comprehensive disaster recovery.

Q: When you say, "more comprehensive disaster recovery," do you have any recovery point objectives (RPO) and recovery time objectives (RTO) defined?

CIO: Yes. We have discussed this internally at length. We realize that we cannot meet the desired RTO and RPO today, which is why we need to discuss this project with you. The RTO for having everything identified for disaster recovery is 24 hours. The RPO will differ depending on the workload. We cannot lose more than 15 minutes worth of some data. On other data, a 24-hour RPO is acceptable.

Q: Is there a defined budget for this project?

CIO: This project is more defined by its goals rather than its budget. We want to do this infrastructure correctly. As long as the expenditure can be justified, we will consider it. Having said that, we do have some relatively new servers that we would like to reuse if possible.

Q: Do you have an existing SAN?

CIO: We do not currently have a SAN.

Q: What are the security requirements for your applications? Can all of the applications being virtualized reside on the same cluster of hosts without additional safeguards to separate their communication among each other?

CIO: All of the targeted applications can reside on the same set of hosts.

NOTE

In this scenario, you will consolidate the applications on the same set of hosts. You might run in to a scenario where network separation is required through virtual firewalls like vShield Zones or the Cisco Virtual Security Gateway or Virtual ASA. You also might be required to physically separate applications into different clusters or by using VM to host affinity rules. It depends on the regulations and customer requirements.

The findings from this conversation are summarized in Table 6.1.

Table 6.1   Crookston and Stagner Bank CIO Interview Findings

Finding	Impact on Design
Bank will be growing both organically and through acquisition.	The infrastructure needs to scale easily with little administrative overhead involved.
There is no real DR in place for the workloads beyond core processing.	DR must be considered as part of the project with defined RPO and RTO.
Customer wants to reuse equipment if possible.	There must be an examination of existing server assets to see where they might fit into the new infrastructure.

Let's set that information aside for later. Now let's look at the planning and design phase of the project.

Planning and Designing

Let's look at the capacity planning data for Crookston and Stagner Bank. As a review, here are the calculations you will be using for 100 physical machines to be converted.

CPU

Average CPU per physical (MHz) × Average CPU count = Normalized average CPU per physical (MHz)

Normalized average CPU per physical (MHz) × Average peak CPU utilization (Percentage) = Average peak CPU utilization (MHz)

CPU requirements for Crookston and Stagner Bank (100 VMs)

3,103MHz × 4 = 12,412MHz

12,412MHz × 16.00% = 1,985.92MHz

Number of concurrent VMs × Average peak CPU utilization (MHz) = CPU (MHz) required for the virtual infrastructure

100 × 1,985.92MHz = 198,592MHz

198,592MHz will be required for this virtual infrastructure.

RAM

Average RAM per physical (MB) × Average peak RAM utilization (Percentage) = Average peak RAM utilization (MB)

Number of concurrent VMs × Average peak RAM utilization (MB) = Total peak RAM utilization (MB)

RAM requirements for Crookston and Stagner Bank (100 VMs)

4,363MB × 55.00% = 2399.65MB

100 × 2399.65MB = 239,965MB

239,965MB will be required for this virtual infrastructure.

Host Specifications

Let's take a look at two host CPU specifications. You will use only 80% of the resources to leave headroom for things like spikes and HA failover scenarios.

Host A CPU

Two 6-core CPU at 2660MHz per core

2 × 6 = 12 × 2660MHz = 31,920MHz

80% × 31,920MHz = 25,536MHz available per host

Host B CPU

Two 10-core CPU at 2400MHz per core

2 × 10 = 20 × 2400MHz = 48,000MHz

80% × 48,000MHz = 38,400MHz available per host

You will use vSphere Enterprise Plus for this infrastructure due to the growth and scalability requirements for the infrastructure. For RAM, let's start with 192GB of RAM for each host because that is the maximum vRAM entitlement given for vSphere Enterprise Plus. Let's do some calculations.

Number of Hosts Needed for CPU Requirements

Total peak CPU utilization (MHz) / CPU (MHZ) available per host = Number of hosts required per CPU requirements (round up)

Number of hosts required per CPU requirements + 1 = Number of hosts required per CPU requirements for N+1 redundancy

> Host A—Number of hosts needed for CPU requirements
>
> 198,592MHz / 25,536MHz = 7.7769 = 8 rounded up
>
> 8 + 1 = 9
>
> 9 hosts are needed for N+1 redundancy.

> Host B—Number of hosts needed for CPU requirements
>
> 198,592MHz / 38,400MHz = 5.1716 = 6 rounded up
>
> 6 + 1 = 7
>
> 7 hosts are needed for N+1 redundancy.

Number of Hosts Needed for RAM Requirements

RAM available per host = RAM per host × 80%

Total peak RAM utilization (MB) / RAM (MB) available per host = Number of hosts required per RAM requirements (round up)

Number of hosts required per RAM requirements + 1 = Number of hosts required per RAM requirements for N+1 redundancy

> 196,608MB × 80% = 157,286.4MB of RAM available per host
>
> 239,965MB / 157,286.4MB = 1.5256 = 2 rounded up
>
> 2 + 1 = 3
>
> 3 hosts are required for N+1 redundancy from a RAM perspective.

The results are summarized in Table 6.2.

Table 6.2 vSphere Infrastructure Requirement Summary

Host	Number of Hosts for CPU	Number of Hosts for RAM
Host A	9	3
Host B	7	3

So, this workload appears to be CPU bound. You have a decision to make. Do you want to scale out or scale up with CPU? We have already discussed the pros and cons of scale up versus scale out. We generally recommend scale up. Also, your CIO interview has given you some more justification for scale up.

One of the primary goals for Crookston and Stagner Bank is consolidation through virtualization. The key word here is consolidation. A higher consolidation ratio is important to the CIO. So, you will choose a scale-up architecture with the fewest amounts of hosts. From a CPU perspective, that means you will go with Host B because only seven are required versus nine hosts for the Host A configuration.

In this case, the RAM requirements do not affect the number of hosts needed. Let's look for the sweet spot where the number of hosts for RAM is closer to the number of hosts needed for CPU. RAM can easily be added to the infrastructure later if it is needed. Let's start with 128GB of RAM.

- **128GB RAM Calculation for Number of Hosts**

- 131,072MB × 80% = 104,857.6MB of RAM available per host

- 239,965MB / 104,857.6MB = 2.2884 = 3 rounded up

- 3 + 1 = 4

- Four hosts are required for N+1 redundancy from a RAM perspective.

This is closer to the 7 hosts required for CPU. Let's look at 64GB of RAM.

- **64GB RAM Calculation for Number of Hosts**

- 65,536MB × 80% = 52,428.8MB of RAM available per host

- 239,965MB / 52,428.8MB = 4.5769 = 5 rounded up

- 5+1 = 6

This is only one host away from the seven hosts required for CPU. You can safely go with 64GB of RAM per host for the initial virtualization. However, for scalability from the start, if the budget permits, you might want to go with more RAM per host. This needs to be considered on a case-by-case basis. Perhaps you should split the difference and go with 128GB of RAM per host in this scenario. So, your chosen host must meet the following CPU and RAM specifications:

Two 10-core CPUs at 2.4GHz per core

128GB of RAM

Next, let's look at networking. Keeping in mind that one of the primary goals for Crookston and Stagner Bank is consolidation, you'll likely want to simplify the infrastructure as well from an equipment perspective. Based on your capacity planning results, you know that the workloads hosted by the server can easily be served by a 1GB network link. So, your networking choice per host will be dictated more by the architecture chosen. To review, let's look at the three general architectures: traditional 1 GbE architecture (see Figure 6.1), converged rackmount architecture (see Figure 6.2), and converged blade architecture (see Figure 6.3).

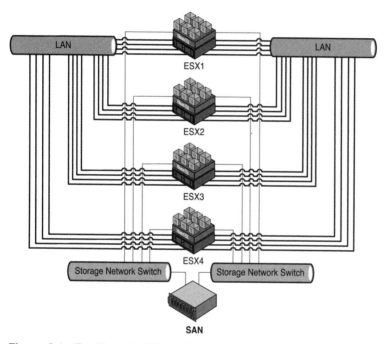

Figure 6.1   Traditional 1 GbE Architecture

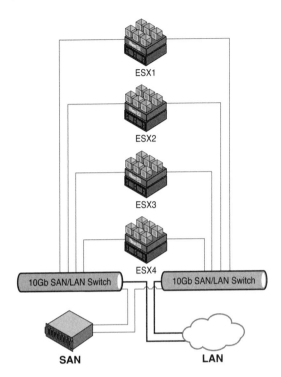

Figure 6.2   Converged Rackmount Architecture

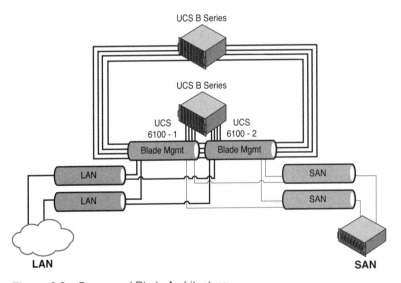

Figure 6.3   Converged Blade Architecture

Let's assume for this scenario that the CIO has indicated that the bank does not want to utilize blades at this time. This leaves the traditional 1GbE architecture and the converged rackmount architecture. Assuming four port group types per host (management, VM, vMotion, IP storage), this would require eight NICs in a traditional 1GbE architecture if you are following traffic isolation and redundancy best practices. A possible port group layout is shown in Figure 6.4.

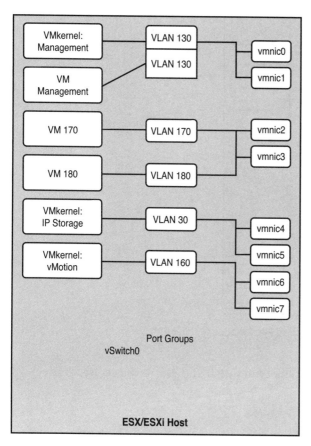

Figure 6.4 Port Group Layout for Traditional 1 GbE Architecture

The converged rackmount architecture would use a two NIC 10GbE layout. The possible port group layout is shown in Figure 6.5.

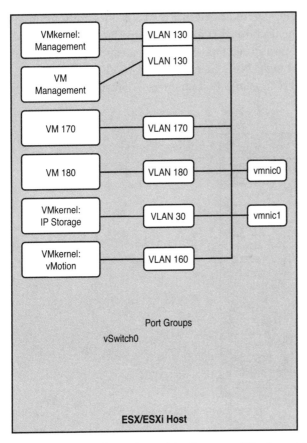

Figure 6.5   Port Group Layout for Converged Rackmount Architecture

Now, let's look at the port count requirements for each of these infrastructure architectures in Table 6.3.

Table 6.3   Port Count by Architecture

Architecture	Number of Hosts	Total Port Count per Switch	Switch Type Needed
1GbE	7	28	48-port 1GbE
Converged rackmount (10GbE)	7	7	24-port 10GbE

The converged rackmount architecture is the clear winner from a port count perspective. It also allows you to gain more bandwidth for your workloads and gives you the option of doing 10GbE iSCSI, NFS, or FCoE FC for the storage protocol.

NOTE

You could also do traditional Fibre Channel here. However, we recommend that new infrastructures that use 10GbE take advantage of storage and network convergence by sending the storage and networking over the same cable.

You will choose the converged rackmount architecture due to the simplicity of management in a converged infrastructure and a decreased port count. You will also use a storage protocol that does not require additional hardware beyond two 10GbE ports.

We recommend using Fibre Channel or FCoE for block-level storage if possible. The Fibre Channel storage protocol is the most stable and most well-understood block storage protocol available. If you will be deploying IP-based storage, then NFS wins for the simplicity with not much additional overhead beyond iSCSI. If you absolutely need IP-based block-level storage, then iSCSI is the clear choice.

For this example, you will use NFS storage. If simplicity is a goal, NFS is going to be the clear winner. Keep in mind that this infrastructure can certainly be added to. For example, you can add dedicated NFS switches later on with additional 10GbE ports on the hosts if you need them. In our experience, this is usually not the case with proper QoS mechanisms in place.

NOTE

We are using NFS here to demonstrate ease of management. However, it is very important to understand the IOPS requirements of the infrastructure before choosing any particular protocol. The design often must balance between ease of management and performance.

The following is the final host specification:

Two 10-core CPUs at 2.4GHz per core

128GB of RAM

One 2-port 10GbE NIC (for added redundancy, two NICs can be added, but only two ports are needed at this time)

Two 73GB 15k hard drives in a mirror for the ESXi installation

Now you have to consider storage. Instead of going through a sizing scenario, like you did in Chapter 1, "Laying the Groundwork," you will review the calculations for the different type of RAID groups here. Each storage vendor will offer differentiators when it comes to storage sizing and performance. Remember that the IOPS for each drive type are as follows:

> 7200 RPM SATA or NL-SAS: 90 IOPS
>
> 15K RPM FC or SAS: 180 IOPS
>
> SSD: 2500

Table 6.4 summarizes the IOPS calculations.

Table 6.4   IOPS Calculations for RAID Types

RAID TYPE	Formula
RAID 5	((Read% + (4 × Write%)) × (IOPS required)) / IOPS per disk = Disk count
RAID 1	((Read% + (2 × Write%)) × (IOPS required)) / IOPS per disk = Disk count

A combination of these IOPS calculations and vendor-specific sizing recommendations will produce a storage recommendation. This combined with the host servers will become the base hardware platform for the infrastructure. Now let's move on to the vSphere design considerations.

We recommend outlining the vSphere decisions made in a table similar to Table 6.5. Here, Table 6.5 also acts as a summary of the decisions you'll make and their justification. A table like Table 6.5 can also be used as implementation documentation.

Table 6.5   vSphere Design Decisions

vSphere Feature	Utilized?	Configuration	Justification
vMotion	Yes	Parallel vMotion	This allows faster time to resolution of DRS load balancing.
DRS	Yes	Fully Automatic/ Moderate	Automatic resolution of load balancing without management overhead.
HA	Yes	Admission Control Enabled/Percentage Based	Automatic recovery of virtual machines. Percentage-based admission control ensures flexibility and control.
FT	No	N/A	FT design considerations do not align with business workflow or workloads.
vCenter	Yes	Virtualized in management cluster	vCenter can take advantage of vSphere features while being isolated from the production workload.

vSphere Feature	Utilized?	Configuration	Justification
Standard vSwitch	Yes	Only on management cluster	The management cluster does not need or have Enterprise Plus licensing to take advantage of distributed switching.
Distributed vSwitch	Yes	Production cluster	There is less management overhead. Can take advantage of NIOC that is necessary for 10GbE converged infrastructure.
Storage DRS	Yes	Capacity only load balancing	The storage uses auto-tiering that is not compatible with latency-based load balancing.
VM Storage Profiles	Yes	User-defined	This enforces compliance for matching RAID type with workload and for protecting DR virtual machines.
vSphere Licensing	Yes	Enterprise Plus for Production/Enterprise for Management	Production will use features like NIOC and vSphere Distributed Switch.
vSphere VNIC Teaming	Yes	Load Based Teaming utilized for production	Originating Port ID will be utilized for the management cluster.

Table 6.5 summarized some of the vSphere design decisions that may need to be made in the infrastructure design process. It is also a good idea to outline the specific parameters in a vSphere design in a document or several tables. These tables will be used by the implementation team to determine how to configure the vSphere infrastructure. The following tables are an example of the specific settings for the scenario. Table 6.6 shows some vSphere naming conventions.

Table 6.6   vSphere Naming Conventions

Attribute	Value
ESXi Hosts	CS-ESX<nn>
vCenter Server	CS-VCENTER<nn>
Datacenter	CS-<purpose>-DC<nn>
Cluster	CS-DC<nn>-<purpose>-CL<nn>
Standard vSwitch	<purpose>-vswitch<nn>
Distributed vSwitch	<purpose>-dvswitch<nn>
Port Groups	<cluster purpose>-<purpose>-<vlan id>
VMFS Datastore	<purpose>-<raid level>-vmfs<nn>
NFS Datastore	<purpose>-<dr for replication>-nfs<nn>

Table 6.7 shows the specific vCenter and VMware Update Manager (VUM) parameters that need to be collected before the implementation.

Table 6.7   vSphere Design vCenter/VUM Parameters

Attribute	Value
vCenter IP/Subnet	192.168.1.10/255.255.255.0
vCenter DNS	CS-VCENTER01
vCenter/VUM DB IP/Subnet	192.168.1.20/255.255.255.0
vCenter/VUM DB DNS IPs	192.168.10.10/192.168.10.20
vCenter/VUM DB DNS	CS-SQL01
vCenter/VUM DB Vendor/Version	Microsoft/SQL 2008 64-Bit
vCenter/VUM DB Authentication	SQL Authentication
vCenter/VUM DB Recovery Method	Full
vCenter/VUM DB Autogrowth	Yes—1MB Increments
vCenter/VUM DB Transaction Log Autogrowth	Yes—10% Increments, Maximum Size—10GB
vCenter Statistics Level	3
Estimated DB Size	10GB
Backup method	Existing backup software SQL agent
vCenter DB Name	CS-VCENTERDB01
VUM DB NAME	CS-VUMDB01
vCenter ODBC System DSN	VCENTERDB
vCenter SQL Account Name/Password/Rights	vcenterdb/P@ssw0rd/dbowner
VUM ODBC System DSN	VUMDB
VUM SQL Account Name/Password/Rights	vcenterdb/P@ssw0rd/dbowner
nter/VUM SQL Client	SQL Native Client

Table 6.8 shows the specific VUM settings for this infrastructure.

Table 6.8   vSphere Design VUM Settings

Attribute	Value
Patch download sources	Select "Download ESX 5 Patches"
Shared repository	D:\VUM

Attribute	Value
Proxy settings	None
Patch download schedule	Every Sunday at 12:00 a.m.
Email notification	helpdesk@candsbank.com
Update Manager baselines	Critical and noncritical ESXi patches/VMware Tools upgrade to match host
ESXi host settings	Host maintenance mode failure: Retry/Retry interval: 30 minutes/Number of retries: 3
vApp settings	Select "Enable smart reboot after remediation"

Table 6.9 shows the general network parameters that need to be collected for Crookston and Stagner Bank.

Table 6.9   vSphere Infrastructure Network Parameters

Attribute	Value
Default gateway	192.168.1.1
NTP server IP	192.168.1.254
DNS IPs	192.168.10.10/192.168.10.20
Storage management IP/mask	. 192.168.1.30/255.255.255.0

Table 6.10 shows the specific host parameters that will be required in the new vSphere infrastructure.

Table 6.10   ESXi Host VMkernel Network Parameters

ESXi Host Name	Management IP/Mask	NFS IP/Mask	vMotion IP/Mask
CS-ESX01	192.168.1.31/255.255.255.0	192.168.20.31/255.255.255.0	192.168.30.31/255.255.255.0
CS-ESX02	192.168.1.32/255.255.255.0	192.168.20.32/255.255.255.0	192.168.30.32/255.255.255.0
CS-ESX03	192.168.1.33/255.255.255.0	192.168.20.33/255.255.255.0	192.168.30.33/255.255.255.0
CS-ESX04	192.168.1.34/255.255.255.0	192.168.20.34/255.255.255.0	192.168.30.34/255.255.255.0
CS-ESX05	192.168.1.35/255.255.255.0	192.168.20.35/255.255.255.0	192.168.30.35/255.255.255.0
CS-ESX06	192.168.1.36/255.255.255.0	192.168.20.36/255.255.255.0	192.168.30.36/255.255.255.0
CS-ESX07	192.168.1.37/255.255.255.0	192.168.20.37/255.255.255.0	192.168.30.37/255.255.255.0

Table 6.11 shows the specific BMC management network parameters.

Table 6.11   ESXi Host Baseboard Management Controller Network Parameters

ESXi Host Name	BMC Management IP/Mask
CS-ESX01	192.168.1.41/255.255.255.0
CS-ESX02	192.168.1.42/255.255.255.0
CS-ESX03	192.168.1.43/255.255.255.0
CS-ESX04	192.168.1.44/255.255.255.0
CS-ESX05	192.168.1.45/255.255.255.0
CS-ESX06	192.168.1.46/255.255.255.0
CS-ESX07	192.168.1.47/255.255.255.0

Table 6.12 shows the monitoring settings for the infrastructure. Hardware components can be monitored through SNMP. vCenter alerts will be triggered and an email will be sent. The ESXi host logs will also be sent to a central syslog server where alarms can be triggered if necessary.

Table 6.12   Monitoring Settings

Attribute	Value
SNMP monitoring server	monitor.candsbank.com
SNMP monitoring server port	162
SNMP community string	commcandsbank
RO community	rocommcandsbank
RW community	rwcommcandsbank
vCenter SMTP server	mail.candsbank.com
vCenter sending account	vcenter@candsbank.com
vCenter receiving account	helpdesk@candsbank.com
Syslog server	syslog.candsbank.com (load balancer)

Table 6.13 shows the various port group names and their associated VLAN IDs that will be used in this infrastructure.

Table 6.13 vSphere Port Group Specifications (Production and Management Cluster)

vSwitch Port Group Name	VLAN ID
prod-dvswitch01 prod-mgmt-130 (vmkernel)	130
prod-dvswitch01 prod-vmmgmt-130 (virtual machine)	130
prod-dvswitch01 prod-vm-170	170
prod-dvswitch01 prod-vm-180	180
prod-dvswitch01 prod-ipstorage-30	30
prod-dvswitch01 prod-vmotion-160	160
mgmt-vswitch01 mgmt-mgmt-130	130
mgmt-vswitch01 mgmt-vmmgmt-130	130
mgmt-vswitch01 mgmt-ipstorage-30	30
mgmt-vswitch01 mgmt-vmotion-160	160

Table 6.14 lists the datastore names and purpose of the storage in the infrastructure.

Table 6.14 Storage Specifications

Datastore Name / NFS Volume Name	LUN ID / Server	Purpose
prod-dr-nfs01 / /vmnfs01	vmnfs.candsbank.com	Production VM—Replicated
prod-dr-nfs02 / /vmnfs02	vmnfs.candsbank.com	Production VM—Replicated
prod-dr-nfs03 / /vmnfs03	vmnfs.candsbank.com	Production VM—Replicated
prod-nfs04 / /vmnfs04	vmnfs.candsbank.com	Production VM—Nonreplicated
prod-nfs05 / /vmnfs05	vmnfs.candsbank.com	Production VM—Nonreplicated
prod-iso-nfs03 / /isonfs02	isonfs.candsbank.com	ISOs and templates

Table 6.15 lists the vSphere roles and permissions that will be required. As this is a small bank, the IT staff typically holds multiple roles (storage, networking, server admin, VM admin). The permissions reflect that. In larger organizations, there may be more separation of roles. Granular, role-based permissions can be assigned using folders in vCenter and should never be assigned using resource pools. Also, the entire vSphere infrastructure from vCenter to the ESXi hosts can now be easily AD integrated as of vSphere 4.1.

Table 6.15   vSphere Roles and Permissions

Role Name	AD Groups	vSphere Privileges	vCenter Inventory Level
VI Admins	VI Admins	Administrator	Root
Helpdesk	Helpdesk	VM Operator	Production VM Folder

Table 6.16 shows the location of any media required for the implementation.

Table 6.16   vSphere Infrastructure Media and Licensing

Media	Location	License Keys Available
ESXi	\\cs-itfile\media\vmware	Yes
vCenter	\\cs-itfile\media\vmware	Yes
OS Media	\\cs-itfile\media\microsoft	Yes
DB Server Media	\\cs-itfile\media\microsoft	Yes

The previous tables served as examples of the kind of information that needs to be gathered as part of the planning and design process. The deployment becomes more efficient if as much information as possible is gathered up front. All of the work that goes into planning will pay off when the time comes to actually implement. Use these tables for every site in the infrastructure. For example, although a detailed discussion of DR with vSphere Site Recovery Manager is beyond the scope of this book, your design requires DR. So, you will need this same type of information relating to the DR site as well.

For ease of management in the event of a production outage, the CIO decided to completely isolate the management infrastructure from the production cluster. Table 6.17 summarizes Crookston and Stagner Bank's new infrastructure.

Table 6.17   vSphere Infrastructure Components

Component	Hardware
vSphere production compute	New host servers
vSphere production storage	New SAN
vSphere production networking	10GbE
vSphere management compute	Reuse existing servers
vSphere management storage	New small SAN
vSphere management networking	1GbE

Component	Hardware
vSphere DR compute	Reuse existing servers
vSphere DR storage	New SAN
vSphere DR networking	10GbE

In addition to the information that you have gathered so far, you should also create a design blueprint in a program like Visio and save it as a PDF. Following is an example of the types of drawings that should be included in this document:

- Cover page with information like table of contents, vSphere version information, and revision history

- Logical cluster overview for each site in the design

- Physical design diagram

- Logical virtual network layout for port groups and upstream switches for each cluster

- Logical SAN layout for each cluster

- Logical LUN/NFS VM layout. This should denote which VMs go on which LUNs/NFS volumes initially

- Logical backup infrastructure diagram

- Logical DR infrastructure diagram

With the information in the previous tables and the design blueprint, the implementation team should be able to install and configure the vSphere infrastructure. This particular design utilizes new servers for the production cluster, reuses servers for management and DR, and utilizes new storage for all three clusters (production, management, and DR). The licensing used at production and DR is Enterprise Plus. This decision was based on the advanced features available like the distributed vSwitch and NIOC that allow the environment to scale more easily. The licensing needed for your own projects will need to be determined by the design requirements. NIOC will be utilized for network QoS to control vMotion, NFS, and general VM traffic. VM Storage Profiles will be utilized to ensure VMs that need to reside on replicated storage are deployed there. Storage DRS will be utilized from a capacity load balancing perspective. This will make it easier when deploying virtual machines. The administrator will not need to determine the free space available on the datastores. Storage DRS will figure it out for the administrator. With the planning and design details taken care of, it is time to move to implementation.

> **NOTE**
>
> The design requires a total of 14 CPU licenses (for seven 2-socket hosts) of vSphere Enterprise Plus. This entitles the infrastructure to 1344GB of vRAM. This is plenty for scaling the RAM as the infrastructure grows. This is another reason Enterprise Plus was chosen. It offers more vRAM per CPU license.

Implementation

After the design documentation has been reviewed, verified, and signed off on, it is time for the implementation. The implementation will follow the following general workflow:

- Verify the design with the design team and stakeholders.

- Gather all of the design documentation and write up an implementation plan, automating processes where possible.

- Decide on a way to handle deviations from the plan.

- Implement the solution.

- Validate the implementation with user acceptance testing of the vSphere features in use.

For this scenario, assume that this workflow has been followed. Two vSphere features that help automate the deployment process are vSphere Auto Deploy and vSphere Host Profiles. These features are discussed in detail in Chapter 2, "Implementing the Solution."

You will utilize vSphere Host Profiles to deploy the infrastructure. A single host will be set up and verified for configuration consistent with the design documentation. This host will serve as the image for your Host Profile. This has the following advantages:

- We are able to quickly deploy hosts.

- A Host Profile ensures configuration consistency within the infrastructure as the deployment continues.

- A Host Profile can be used to ensure ongoing configuration consistency after the deployment.

Verifying every aspect of the design up front is very important because a misconfiguration has a cascading effect when using deployment automation. This is why we provided the details in the tables as part of the planning and design phase. As an added precaution, these documents can be placed in a revision control system and only checked out when needed.

After the implementation, the functionality of the infrastructure is verified. Only after this verification and customer acceptance can you begin deploying virtual machines to the infrastructure. After all of the physical to virtual migrations and virtual machine deployments have been done, you can begin operating the new infrastructure for Crookston and Stagner Bank.

Operating

The infrastructure at Crookston and Stagner Bank has been implemented. Now you must operate the infrastructure on a day-to-day basis. This is where all of the planning and documentation in the design and implementation phases can really pay dividends. A well-structured infrastructure is easier to operate than one that was just thrown together. Even items like naming conventions can make the environment much easier to operate and troubleshoot.

Chapter 3, "Operating the Environment," covered many of the aspects of operating the infrastructure. This section highlights some important notes from Chapter 3 that apply to any infrastructure. Following are some of the tasks that will take place when operating the infrastructure on a day-to-day basis. Be sure to have a documented procedure for performing these items and use automation whenever possible for task consistency.

- Patching the infrastructure components (ESX hosts, host firmware, vCenter, switching firmware, storage firmware, and OS patches)

- Setting up and responding to infrastructure alarms

- Backing up and recovering infrastructure components and virtual machines

- Deploying new virtual machines and performing physical to virtual migrations

For Crookston and Stagner Bank, you have developed a patch schedule for the infrastructure components. After some time, you have also set up appropriate infrastructure alarms. The backup of virtual machines will be handled with multiple methods. Image-level backups will be handled by the existing backup vendor's virtual machine–specific module. File-level backups will also be taken for certain virtual machines using the traditional backup module in the existing backup software. The backup target will be disk based for fast recovery. Those backups will be replicated to a similar disk-based backup target at the DR site. Figure 6.6 shows a sample diagram of this infrastructure.

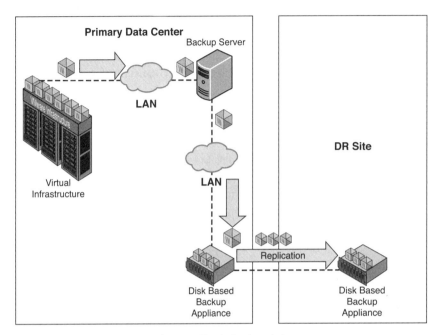

Figure 6.6   Crookston and Stagner Bank Backup Infrastructure

A health check script will be run on a daily basis to check for items like old virtual machine snapshots. Snapshots can be taken manually or they can be taken automatically by our virtual machine–specific backup software. A virtual machine snapshot can be problematic as it can grow to the size of its original virtual hard drive (VMDK) file. This can cause capacity and performance problems, as shown in Chapter 3. We mention them here again as they are the most common problems we see in infrastructures when we perform health checks. The following guidelines apply to virtual machine snapshots:

- Snapshots are useful before a virtual machine OS is patched and should be deleted shortly afterward.

- Generally, a snapshot should not be kept for any more than 48 hours. There may be a business requirement to keep them longer, but they should be monitored.

- Snapshots are not backups. They are meant to be used for a temporary point in time recovery.

- The infrastructure should be checked on a frequent basis for old snapshots. They can quickly fill up a datastore and cause performance degradation and outages if not monitored.

Operating the infrastructure should be easier if the vSphere features are fully utilized. Let the infrastructure work for you instead of you working for the infrastructure. Utilize DRS and Storage DRS for automated load balancing and virtual machine placement. Use vSphere HA for an automated reboot of workloads should a host fail. Utilize scripting and automation whenever possible to ensure an efficient and consistent operating environment.

Although operating the environment is the majority of what you will be doing on a day-to-day basis at Crookston and Stagner Bank, you will also need to manage the new infrastructure. This is also where proper planning up front will help in the long run.

Managing

Let's take a look at how some of your design decisions have positively impacted the management of the new virtual infrastructure at Crookston and Stagner Bank in Table 6.18.

Table 6.18 Design Decision Benefit

Design Decision	Impact
Scale-up infrastructure	This choice will allow us to save money on licensing and management overhead due to less hardware.
Converged rackmount architecture	10GbE gives more bandwidth with fewer switch ports. The infrastructure cabling is dramatically simplified.
vSphere distributed switch	QoS and NIOC can be used for traffic management. Netflow can be used for troubleshooting.
Load Based Teaming	Truly dynamic load balancing is accomplished to most effectively take advantage of the 10GbE infrastructure investment.
vCenter as VM	This choice allows the failover and rapid recovery for vCenter itself.
Management cluster	Management of the infrastructure is isolated from the infrastructure it is managing. This allows faster management recovery should a failure occur.
Multiprotocol array chosen	This choice will allow flexible protocol choice for the future if needed.
VAAI- and VASA-capable array	Should block storage be utilized in the future, the array is ready. Storage capabilities can be presented to the VMware administrator through vCenter.
No resource pools/no limits or shares	This makes the infrastructure easier to troubleshoot. This feature can be added later if needed.

The vCenter Operations management suite will also be added to the new infrastructure. This will ensure proactive forecasting of resource need. This tool is also invaluable for quickly diagnosing performance bottlenecks in the infrastructure without searching through vCenter or using command-line tools in the hosts or other hardware.

Full Case Study Summary

This case study has demonstrated how design decisions early on can impact the operation and management of the infrastructure later. It is important to plan as much as possible so that there can be a smooth transition between building and operating the infrastructure. The following are the main takeaways to keep in mind when building a virtual infrastructure:

- Plan ahead of time. This should be the longest phase of the project.

- Consider the design requirements, assumptions, and constraints and use them to guide your design decisions.

- Consider the impact of each design decision.

- Gather as many details as possible on every aspect of the design before starting the implementation to avoid bottlenecks and questions when it comes time to implement.

- Use built-in tools and features as well as third-party tools and features to automate as much as possible in the implementation, operation, and management of the infrastructure.

- Proactively monitor the infrastructure for resource usage to better forecast when more resources will be needed. This will make the budget conversation much easier.

Virtual infrastructures are complex because they touch every aspect of the organization. When workloads are virtualized, the datacenter is consolidated to a handful of hardware components. This also consolidates risk, so planning and consistent execution is paramount in the success of the virtualization project. If this advice is followed, the organization can reap many more of the benefits of virtualization and work toward achieving a dynamic, efficient, and resilient 100% virtualized infrastructure.

Additional Resources

Chapter 2: Implementing the Solution

PowerCLI:

http://www.Virtualizeplanet.com—Excellent source of lessons

http://www.Virtu-al.net—Great repository of scripts and further training

http://www.Lucd.info

Auto Deploy:

VMware in their *VMware vSphere 5.0 Evaluation Guide, Volume Four*:

http://www.vmware.com/files/pdf/products/vsphere/VMware-vSphere-Evaluation-Guide-4-Auto-Deploy.pdf

Configuration options for High Availability:

Duncan Epping's HA Deepdive: http://www.yellow-bricks.com/vmware-high-availability-deepdiv/

A scripted resource to test vMotion:

http://communities.vmware.com/docs/DOC-17941

Fault tolerance considerations and requirements:

VMware Knowledge Base article 1013428:

http://kb.vmware.com/kb/1013428

Esxtop learning resource:

http://communities.vmware.com/docs/DOC-11812

Resource for verifying NFS connectivity still exists to the host:

VMware Knowledge Base article 1003728:

http://kb.vmware.com/kb/1003728

Configuring iSCSI port binding refer to the vSphere Storage Guide:

http://pubs.vmware.com/vsphere-50/topic/com.vmware.ICbase/PDF/vsphere-esxi-vcenter-server-50-storage-guide.pdf

PowerPath and the best practices for using it in your vSphere environment:

http://www.emc.com/collateral/software/white-papers/h6340-powerpath-ve-for-vmware-vsphere-wp.pdf

Using esxtop to check disk metrics for each host:
http://communities.vmware.com/docs/DOC-11812

VMware Knowledge Base article 1008205:

http://kb.vmware.com/kb/1008205

Running a health check yourself:

http://communities.vmware.com/docs/DOC-9842

Portfast

VMware Knowledge Base article 1003804:

http://kb.vmware.com/kb/1003804

Why auto-negotiation is recommended:

VMware Knowledge Base article 1004089

http://kb.vmware.com/kb/1004089

Chapter 3: Operating the Environment

PowerShell script for finding snapshots:

http://www.lucd.info/2010/03/31/uml-diagram-your-vm-vdisks-and-snapshots/

PowerGUI:

http://www.powergui.org

VMware Knowledge Base article 1025279:

http://kb.vmware.com/kb/1025279

Alarms:

VMware Knowledge Base article 1018029:

http://kb.vmware.com/kb/1018029

Required ports to be allowed through a firewall:

VMware Knowledge Base article 1010056:

http://kb.vmware.com/kb/1010056

PowerShell Script for easy configuration of alarms

You can download this script from http://www.seancrookston.com/set_alarms.ps1

Daily health check: vCheck:

http://www.virtu-al.net/featured-scripts/vcheck/

Health check advantages:

http://www.vmware.com/files/pdf/services/consserv-vmware-vsphere-health-check-datasheet.pdf

Chapter 4: Managing the Environment

EVC baselines and CPU compatibility:

VMware Knowledge Base article 1003212:

http://kb.vmware.com/kb/1003212

Configuration maximums for vSphere 5:

http://www.vmware.com/pdf/vsphere5/r50/vsphere-50-configuration-maximums.pdf

Sample configurations for etherchannel:

VMware Knowledge Base article 1004048:

http://kb.vmware.com/kb/1004048

IP-Hash calculations:

VMware Knowledge Base article 1007371:

http://kb.vmware.com/kb/1007371

ESX host network flapping error when beacon probing is selected:

VMware Knowledge Base article 1012819:

http://kb.vmware.com/kb/1012819

Cisco Nexus 1000v Data Sheet:
http://www.cisco.com/en/US/prod/collateral/switches/ps9441/ps9902/data_sheet_c78-492971.html

VMware Compatibility Guide:

http://www.vmware.com/resources/compatibility/search.php?deviceCategory=san

Chapter 5: Roadblocks to 100% Virtualization

Deploying a virtual desktop environment:

View 5 Architecture and Planning Guide:

http://pubs.vmware.com/view-50/topic/com.vmware.ICbase/PDF/view-50-architecture-planning.pdf

View WAN reference architecture:

http://www.vmware.com/files/pdf/view_wan_reference_architecture.pdf

VMware View 5: Building a Successful Virtual Desktop by Paul O'doherty

Networking virtualization:

http://www.cisco.com/en/US/solutions/collateral/ns340/ns517/ns224/ns892/ns894/white_paper_c11-525307.html

Capital and operational expenditures:

http://www.techyv.com/article/opex-capex-are-two-major-terms-asset-or-resource-management-system

Potential issues with CPU affinity:

http://pubs.vmware.com/vsphere-esx-4-1/wwhelp/wwhimpl/js/html/
wwhelp.htm#context=resmgmt&file=c_potential_issues_with_cpu_affinity.html

License chart:

http://www.vmware.com/products/vsphere/buy/editions_comparison.html

Index

M

N

W-X-Y-Z

  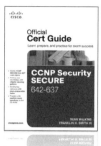  

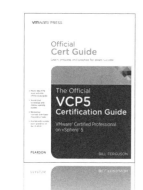

Managing and Optimizing VMware vSphere® Deployments

IT BEST PRACTICES

Sean Crookston
Harley Stagner

FREE
Online Edition

Your purchase of *Managing and Optimizing VMware vSphere Deployments* includes access to a free online edition for 45 days through the **Safari Books Online** subscription service. Nearly every VMware Press book is available online through **Safari Books Online**, along with thousands of books and videos from publishers such as Addison-Wesley Professional, Cisco Press, Exam Cram, IBM Press, O'Reilly Media, Prentice Hall, Que, and Sams.

Safari Books Online is a digital library providing searchable, on-demand access to thousands of technology, digital media, and professional development books and videos from leading publishers. With one monthly or yearly subscription price, you get unlimited access to learning tools and information on topics including mobile app and software development, tips and tricks on using your favorite gadgets, networking, project management, graphic design, and much more.

Activate your FREE Online Edition at
informit.com/safarifree

STEP 1: Enter the coupon code: HMIHFAA.

STEP 2: New Safari users, complete the brief registration form.
Safari subscribers, just log in.

If you have difficulty registering on Safari or accessing the online edition,
please e-mail customer-service@safaribooksonline.com

 Addison Wesley AdobePress ALPHA Cisco Press FT Press IBM Press Microsoft Press New Riders O'REILLY

 Peachpit Press PRENTICE HALL que Redbooks  SAMS SAS Publishing vmware PRESS WILEY wrox